DEMOCRACY

The Greatest Good for the Greatest Number

Edited and with an Introduction by
Maryann Zihala

University Press of America,® Inc.
Lanham · Boulder · New York · Toronto · Oxford

Copyright © 2003 by
University Press of America,® Inc.
4501 Forbes Boulevard
Suite 200
Lanham, Maryland 20706
UPA Acquisitions Department (301) 459-3366

PO Box 317
Oxford
OX2 9RU, UK

ISBN 0-7618-2618-1 (paperback : alk. ppr.)

CONTENTS:

	Introduction	1
I.	Jean Jacques Rousseau The Social Contract	9
II.	John Locke Second Treatise of Government	17
III.	James Madison Federalist Paper #10	34
IV.	Alexis de Tocqueville Democracy in America	44
V.	Aristotle The Politics	62
VI.	Thomas Aquinas The Governance of Rulers	85
VII.	Marcus Cicero On the Laws	94
VIII.	John Stuart Mill On Representative Government	101
IX.	Horace Mann Report on the Public Schools	119
X.	Adam Smith The Wealth of Nations	126
XI.	Karl Marx & Frederick Engels The Communist Manifesto	141
XII.	Andrew Carnegie The Gospel of Wealth	159
	Index	165

"The advantage of democracy does not consist...
in favoring the prosperity of all,
but simply in contributing to the well-being
of the greatest number."

Alexis de Toqueville

Introduction

Democracy is often referred to as the governing system that will give us the greatest good for the greatest number. Government, politics, society, culture, and economy all need to be concerned with the greatest good for the greatest number. Enlightened self-interest causes individuals to pursue that which will bring to them the greatest success, the greatest pleasure, and the most profit. When individuals maximize their resources to bring the most happiness to themselves, a society is created that, as a whole, maximizes its resources. Benjamin Franklin once said: "When you are good to others, you are best to yourself." One could just as easily say that when you are best to yourself, you are also good to others: a rising tide lifts all boats.

In a capitalist economy, these same rules apply. Indeed, in many ways capitalism and democracy seem to have a symbiotic relationship. Is it even possible to have one without the other? Of course it is and we have many examples of one without the other. However, having one almost always leads to the creation of the other. Capitalism and democracy combined bring the greatest level of prosperity to all members of a society. In this light we see that the whole is greater than the sum of its parts.

Francis Fukuyama's world-renowned essay, *The End of History?* (1989), outlined this when he argued that the fall of communism and the end of the Cold War might very well signal that the ideological evolution of mankind is over; we have reached our pinnacle and proven that the best system is liberal democracy and capitalism.

"What we may be witnessing is...the end of history as such: that is, the end point of mankind's ideological evolution and the universalization of Western liberal democracy as the final form of human government...The victory of liberalism has occurred primarily in the realm of ideas or consciousness and is as yet incomplete in the real or material world. But there are powerful reasons for believing that it is the ideal that will govern the material world in the long run.

"Hegel believed that history culminated in an absolute moment—a moment in which a final, rational form of society and state became victorious...The state that emerges at the end of history is liberal insofar as it recognizes and protects, through a system of law, man's universal right to freedom, and democratic government insofar as it exists only with the consent of the governed."[1]

It is important to explain at this point the difference between the modern definition of liberal and the classic definition of liberal; there is a difference. In our sense today, being liberal means advocating a large federal government with significant involvement in many aspects of social and economic policy. That is not the classic definition of liberal and does not apply to the concept of liberal democracy that we are discussing here. In our context we are referring to the

---

[1] Francis Fukuyama, The End of History? <u>The New Shape of World Politics</u>, (Foreign Affairs, New York, 1997), pp. 2-3.

idea that government is designed to provide for the common welfare and the common defense and should otherwise leave citizens alone to pursue their own life, liberty, and happiness. This treatise seeks to explore the ideas of those who believe that the best type of government for that purpose is a democratic one that can provide only that which is necessary and leave the rest to private individuals.

Yet, this type of liberal democracy is not to be confused with a pure majoritarian system. That implies a type of direct democracy that does not always concern itself with the rights of the minority. There are several essays contained here that address the excesses of that type of system. The discussion here centers on the idea of giving the majority that which it wants without denying the minority a say in the process.

Claes Ryn, in his book, *Democracy and the Ethical Life*, explains this well. "An ethical theory of democracy looks for more in the celebrated principle of majority rule than the idea that a numerically superior portion of a people is entitled to greater influence over public decisions than a numerically inferior one."[2]

Dr. Ryn advocates constitutional democracy as the way to allow the will of the majority to be expressed while ensuring minority rights, but also saving us from ourselves. "The idea of constitutional democracy...can be viewed as implying a recognition on the part of the people that there is a need to protect ourselves from our own spontaneity in politics...a people may recognize the need for putting brakes on its own momentary will in the interest of the common good."[3] This is sometimes referred to as the difference between public opinion versus popular opinion. Public opinion is widespread and deep-seated; popular opinion is faddish and changes on a whim. In any type of system, governing based on popular opinion is unwise at best and dangerous at worst. A written constitution sets the parameters—the rules and regulations—so that a democratic political system can avoid degenerating into a tyranny of the majority.

Following is a collection of essays by some of the greatest minds the world has ever known, each giving his thoughts on

---

[2] Claes G. Ryn, <u>Democracy and the Ethical Life</u>, (Catholic University of America Press, Washington, D.C., 1990), pg. 10.
[3] Ibid., pp. 15-16.

a particular aspect of democracy. These essays look at democracy and its impact on a society from many different angles including majoritarianism, representative government, law and justice, capitalism, communism, enlightened self-interest, and education. This collection of philosophical essays begins with some of those who have given us our basic concepts of democratic government—what it should be and what it should do and the best structure for achieving the greatest good for the greatest number.

Jean Jacques Rousseau outlined the idea of the social contract and the need to sacrifice the individual will for the greater good. John Locke added to that the ideas of natural rights, which are to be protected by government, and the consent of the governed, which is necessary in order for a government to have legitimacy. When government loses that consent by failing to honor the social contract, it is the right of the governed to replace that government.

Locke was one of those considered to be a philosopher of the Enlightenment—arguably the greatest of the 'enlightened' philosophers. This was a time period in the history of western thought when representative democracy was being considered as an alternative to monarchy and aristocracy. This is also sometimes called the 'Age of Reason' and was known for applying Isaac Newton's laws of the universe to man and government. If the universe is an ordered, reasonable place, then so is man and the 'divine right of kings' may need some reconsideration. Science and reason were coming to the fore and religion and royalty were both being challenged.

John Stuart Mill would probably find that he had much in common with James Madison. Both believed in the concept of democracy but both also believed in representative democracy. They would also both agree that the best and the brightest should be the ones who rule. Madison's representative democracy—in the form of our U.S. Constitution—would be less likely to allow a tyranny of the majority than would direct democracy. By exercising power through representatives elected by the people, the interests of all portions of society get a fair hearing. This is similar to the philosophy of Aristotle in that he too believed that the majority, ruling through a system of direct democracy, would always harbor the possibility of ignoring the wishes of what might frequently be 49 percent of the population.

While Americans did not invent democracy, it is safe to say that we re-invented it—in the modern sense—some 2000 years after the fall of the city-states of ancient Greece. The French philosopher, Alexis de Toqueville, visited America shortly after its birth to observe this 'new' system of government first hand. He allowed—as did Winston Churchill once[4]—that while democracy may not be the best system, it certainly is a good one. "The advantage of democracy does not consist...in favoring the prosperity of all, but simply in contributing to the well-being of the greatest number." Toqueville, an aristocrat himself, foresaw the inevitable advance of popular government and, like others, worried of the possibility of a direct democracy degenerating into a tyranny of the majority over the minority.

Toqueville traveled to America when the idea of Jacksonian democracy was just taking hold. Jeffersonian republicanism, and its somewhat elitist underpinnings, was waning and more of the citizens—the common people—were participating in the political process than ever before. It would still be some time until all citizens would be able to participate, but by the 1830s most of the property requirements for voting had been removed or reduced to an inconsequential amount. Jeffersonian republicanism had allowed for rule by the people, albeit indirectly through elected representatives. Now we were seeing an increase in the number of people eligible to participate in those elections and stand for election themselves. Jeffersonian republicanism allowed that only the best and the brightest should rule, but that anyone should have the opportunity to rise to the top. From the beginning, America had a class system that allowed social mobility based on hard work and success rather than on wealth, family, and birthright. Now more people were partaking of the opportunities that would help them succeed.

Toqueville observed that this increase in participation would lead to majoritarianism, which would carry with it the possibility of taking away freedom and liberty if left

---

[4] Churchill once opined that democracy was the worst political system—"except for all the others."

unchecked. In a democracy the freedom of the minority is sometimes sacrificed to the will of the majority. On this point, Mill would have agreed with him.

But as Dr. Fukuyama noted: "The egalitarianism of modern America represents the essential achievement of the classless society envisioned by Marx. This is not to say that there are not rich people and poor people in the United States, or that the gap between them has not grown in recent years. But the root causes of economic inequality do not have to do with the underlying legal and social structure of our society, which remains fundamentally egalitarian and moderately redistributionist, so much as with the cultural and social characteristics of the groups that make it up..."[5]

Toqueville would find that interesting. He pointed out that the growing majoritarianism that he could see in America would eventually create a society so equal that everyone would seem the same, have the same ideas, and enjoy the same things.

Horace Mann's essay on education and its value to the masses is included here because one common thread among these thinkers is that the people must have information and knowledge in order to be able to participate in any democratic system. In this we see some of the elitism that they might be accused of advocating. However, again, all people can gain the necessary knowledge to make decisions and rise to the position of being elected officials who represent the people and govern, but it takes education to reach that epoch. The people must be educated if they are to make informed decisions. Indeed, J.S. Mill would not have allowed illiterate people to vote at all. His voting requirement would be literacy, not property. Aristotle thought education taught not just how to rule but how to be ruled. He considered education to be, quite possibly, the single most important thing for a society. As did Thomas Jefferson, who once opined that the people will make the right choices if they are given enough information. "I know of no safe depository of the ultimate powers of the society but the people themselves, and if we think them not enlightened enough to exercise their control with a wholesome discretion, the remedy is not to take it from

---

[5] Fukuyama, pg. 11.

them but to inform their discretion by education." John Locke considered us to be born as clean slates upon which life's experiences would write. In that way, we were all born equal.

The necessity of the "rule of law" is another common thread among these thinkers. Although the concentration here is on majoritarian democracy, the rule of law is an important part of that type of political system. Without the rule of law, with a system of justice that is arbitrary, there is no fairness, no expectation of retribution toward lawbreakers, and no fear that prevents criminal behavior. This eventually leads to chaos and anarchy. As Cicero noted, "License is wont to prevail when there is too little to fear."

Thomas Aquinas, who seems to prefer the rule of a monarch to a democratic system, also preferred a benevolent monarch because, he opined, tyrants rule arbitrarily for their own personal gain and not for the good of society as a whole. A good king, he said, rules for the common good.

J.S. Mill's reason for having laws reinforces his belief that the people should always be able to make their own decisions, within reason and with limits. He believed that people are free to do what they want until what they do affects someone else's liberty. "As soon as any part of a person's conduct affects prejudicially the interests of others, society has jurisdiction over it."

Jefferson considered the rule of law to be of paramount importance to a society and he believed the American people recognized this. "That love of order and obedience to the laws, which so remarkably characterizes the citizens of the United States, are sure pledges of internal tranquility; and the elective franchise, if guarded as the ark of our safety, will peaceably dissipate all combinations to subvert a Constitution dictated by the wisdom and resting on the will of the people. That will is the only legitimate foundation of any government, and to protect its free expression should be our first object."

The final essays contained here address the economic aspect of achieving the greatest good for the greatest number with a comparison of capitalism versus communism. Communism is based on the idea that one should give according to ability and take according to need. Here we have the father of communism, Karl Marx, being challenged by one of the greatest capitalist theorists ever, Adam Smith.

Karl Marx was a German philosopher who synthesized several ideas into what we know as Marxism: German philosophy, French socialism, and British economics. Indeed, he was known to have read Adam Smith's *Wealth of Nations*. Smith theorized about the virtues of capitalism; Marx theorized that capitalism would ultimately fail. Smith believed that capitalism would bring the greatest good to the greatest number. Marx believed that communism—a socialist utopian system—was what would provide the greatest good for the greatest number.

In many ways, Andrew Carnegie, one of the 'Captains of Industry' in the 19th century, synthesized the ideas of both men. He extolled the best of the capitalist system and lambasted the worst of it. In his 'Gospel of Wealth,' Carnegie allows that even if enlightened self-interest helps to bring a certain level of prosperity to most people, it is still the obligation of the capitalists (the wealthy) to provide for those who do not receive benefit from the system. And in this combination Carnegie sees the greatest good for the greatest number; capitalism takes care of most and the capitalists take care of the rest.

Of all the systems that have been tried, only democracy has lasted and been proven to be the one system that can provide the greatest good for the greatest number. And while we can find many faults with democratic systems of government, there is none that has ever been found to be better. It is the only system that fulfills the needs of most people.

I. Jean Jacques Rousseau:
The Social Contract

Jean Jacques Rousseau (1712 1778) was born in Geneva and is credited with three revolutionary ideas in Western thought: civilization is not a good thing, instinct is better than reason, and citizens should be subordinate to the will of the whole. It is this last point that concerns us here.

Rousseau's Social Contract, written in 1762, is often cited as being the most influential treatise on the concept of democratic self-government. Rousseau believed that by nature men are free and by nature mankind is good. Indeed, Rousseau opines that it is man's freedom that makes him moral. "For to take away all freedom from his will is to take away all morality from his actions."

Men left the state of nature behind and banded together willingly in order to create some orderly form of society with the authority to rule for the good of the whole. Individuals willingly surrendered some of their liberties to this body politic. "As soon as the act of association becomes a reality, it substitutes for a person of each of the contracting parties a moral and collective body made up of as many members as the constituting assembly has votes, which body receives from this very act of constitution its unity, its dispersed self, and its will. The public person thus formed by the union of individuals was known in the old days as a City, but now as the Republic or Body Politic."

The 'social contract' created a collective body of the people who would act as a whole for the good of the whole. No one person would ever be subordinated to another because they were all part of the same whole. The people, as a collective body or body politic, are sovereign and have the ability to exercise the 'general will.' "Only the general will can direct the forces of the state according to the purpose for which it was instituted, which is the common good… For it is utterly on the basis of the common interest that society ought to be governed."

Rousseau believed that the 'general will' could be determined by having the people all come together to vote on whatever might be best for the whole, and then leave the implementation to someone else—a government body or administrator of some sort. To Rousseau this would not be representative democracy but direct democracy. The government would only do what it was instructed to do by the body politic. This is a position somewhere between those taken by Thomas Hobbes and John Locke—the former preferring to give more authority to the government with the latter preferring to give very little power to the government.

Jean Jacques Rousseau: The Social Contract

Whether The General Will Is Fallible

It follows from what has gone before that the general will is always right and tends to the public advantage; but it does not follow that the deliberations of the people are always equally correct. Our will is always for our own good, but we do not always see what that is; the people is never corrupted, but it is often deceived, and on such occasions only does it seem to will what is bad.

There is often a great deal of difference between the will of all and the general will; the latter considers only the common interest, while the former takes private interest into account, and is no more than a sum of particular wills: but take away from these same wills the pluses and minuses that cancel one another, and the general will remains as the sum of the differences.

If, when the people, being furnished with adequate information, held its deliberations, the citizens had no communication one with another, the grand total of the small differences would always give the general will, and the decision would always be good. But when factions arise, and partial associations are formed at the expense of the great association, the will of each of these associations becomes general in relation to its members, while it remains particular in relation to the State: it may then be said that there are no longer as many votes as there are men, but only as many as there are associations. The differences become less numerous and give a less general result. Lastly, when one of these associations is so great as to prevail over all the rest, the result is no longer a sum of small differences, but a single difference; in this case there is no longer a general will, and the opinion which prevails is purely particular.

It is therefore essential, if the general will is to be able to express itself, that there should be no partial society within the State, and that each citizen should think only his own thoughts... But if there are partial societies, it is best to have as many as possible and to prevent them from being unequal... These precautions are the only ones that can guarantee that the general will shall be always enlightened, and that the people shall in no way deceive itself.

That The General Will Is Indestructible

As long as several men in assembly regard themselves as a single body, they have only a single will, which is concerned with their common preservation and general well being. In this case, all the springs of the State are vigorous and simple and its rules clear and luminous; there are no embroilments or conflicts of interests; the common good is everywhere clearly apparent, and only good sense is needed to perceive it. Peace, unity, and equality are the enemies of political subtleties. Men who are upright and simple are difficult to deceive because of their simplicity; lures and ingenious pretexts fail to impose upon them, and they are not even subtle enough to be dupes. When, among the happiest people in the world, bands of peasants are seen regulating affairs of State under an oak, and always acting wisely, can we help scorning the ingenious methods of other nations, which make themselves illustrious and wretched with so much art and mystery?

A State so governed needs very few laws; and, as it becomes necessary to issue new ones, the necessity is universally seen. The first man to propose them merely says what all have already felt, and there is no question of factions or intrigues or eloquence in order to secure the passage into law of what every one has already decided to do, as soon as he is sure that the rest will act with him.

Theorists are led into error because, seeing only States that have been from the beginning wrongly constituted, they are struck by the impossibility of applying such a policy to them. They make great game of all the absurdities a clever rascal or an insinuating speaker might get the people of Paris or London to believe...

But when the social bond begins to be relaxed and the State to grow weak, when particular interests begin to make themselves felt and the smaller societies to exercise an influence over the larger, the common interest changes and finds opponents: opinion is no longer unanimous; the general will ceases to be the will of all; contradictory views and debates arise; and the best advice is not taken without question.

Finally, when the State, on the eve of ruin, maintains only a vain, illusory and formal existence, when in every heart the social bond is broken, and the meanest interest brazenly lays hold of the sacred name of "public good," the general will becomes mute: all men, guided by secret motives, no more give their views as citizens than if the State had never been; and iniquitous decrees directed solely to private interest get passed under the name of laws.

Does it follow from this that the general will is exterminated or corrupted? Not at all: it is always constant, unalterable and pure; but it is subordinated to other wills, which encroach upon its sphere. Each man, in detaching his interest from the common interest, sees clearly that he cannot entirely separate them, but his share in the public mishaps seems to him negligible beside the exclusive good he aims at making his own. Apart from this particular good, he wills the general good in his own interest, as strongly as any one else. Even in selling his vote for money, he does not extinguish in himself the general will, but only eludes it. The fault he commits is that of changing the state of the question, and answering something different from what he is asked. Instead of saying by his vote, "It is to the advantage of the State," he says, "It is of advantage to this or that man or party that this or that view should prevail." Thus the law of public order in assemblies is not so much to maintain in them the general will as to secure that the question be always put to it, and the answer always given by it.

I could here set down many reflections on the simple right of voting in every act of Sovereignty—a right which no one can take from the citizens—and also on the right of stating views, making proposals, dividing and discussing, which the government is always most careful to leave solely to its members, but this important subject would need a treatise to itself, and it is impossible to say everything in a single work.

On Voting

It is clear from the preceding chapter that the manner in which general business is taken care of can provide a rather accurate indication of the present state of mores and of the health of the body politic. The more harmony reigns in the assemblies, that is to say the closer opinions come to unanimity, the more dominant too is the general will. But long debates, dissentions, and tumult betoken the ascendance of private interests and the decline of the state.

This seems less evident when two or more orders enter into its constitution, as had been done in Rome by the patricians and the plebeians, whose quarrels often disturbed the comitia, even in the best of times in the Republic. But this exception is more apparent than real. For then, by the vice inherent in the body politic, there are, as it were, two states in one.

What is not true of the two together is true of each of them separately. And indeed often in the most tumultuous times, the plebiscite of the people, when the senate did not interfere with them, always passed quietly and by a large majority of votes. Since the citizens have but one interest, the people had but one will.

At the other extreme of the circle, unanimity returns. It is when the citizens, having fallen into servitude, no longer have either liberty or will. Then fear and flattery turn voting into acclamations. People no longer deliberate, either they adore or they curse. Such was the vile manner in which the senate expressed its opinions under the emperors; sometimes it did so with ridiculous precautions. Tacitus observes that under Otho, the senators, while heaping curses upon Vitellius, contrived at the same time to make a frightening noise so that, if by chance he became master, he would be unable to know what each of them had said.

From these various considerations there arise the maxims by which the manner of counting votes and comparing opinions should be regulated, depending on whether the general will is more or less easy to know and the state, more or less in decline.

There is but one law that by its nature requires unanimous consent. This is the social compact. For civil association is the most voluntary act in the world. Since every man is born free and master of himself, no one can, under any pretext whatever, place another under subjection without his consent. To decide that the son of a slave is born a slave is to decide that he was not a man.

If, therefore, at the time of the social compact there are opponents to it, their opposition does not invalidate the contract; it merely prevents them from being included in it. They are foreigners among citizens. Once the state is instituted, residency implies consent. To inhabit the territory is to submit to sovereignty. Aside from this primitive contract, the vote of the majority always obligates all the others. This is the consequence of the contract itself.

But it is asked how a man can be both free and forced to conform to wills that are not his own. How can the opponents be both free and be placed in subjugation to laws to which they have not consented? I answer that the question is not put properly. The citizen consents to all the laws, even to those that pass in spite of his opposition, and even to those that punish him when he dares to violate any of them. The constant will of all the members of the state is the general will; through it they are citizens and free. When a law is proposed in the people's assembly, what is asked of them is not precisely whether they approve or reject, but whether or not it conforms to the general will that is theirs. Each man, in giving his vote, states his opinion on this matter and the declaration of the general will is drawn from the counting of votes. When, therefore, the opinion contrary to mine prevails, this proves merely that I was in error and that what I took to be the general will was not so. If my private opinion had prevailed, I would have done something other than what I had wanted. In that case I would not have been free. This presupposes, it is true, that all the characteristics of the general will are still in the majority. When they cease to be free, there is no longer any liberty regardless of the side one takes.

In showing earlier how private wills were substituted for the general will in public deliberations, I have given an adequate indication of the possible ways of preventing this abuse. I will discuss this again at a later time. With respect to the proportional number of votes needed to declare this will, I have also given the principles on the basis of which it can be determined. The difference of a single vote breaks a tie vote; a single opponent destroys a unanimous vote. But between a unanimous and a tie vote there are several unequal divisions, at any of which this proportionate number can be fixed in accordance with the condition and needs of the body politic.

Two general maxims can serve to regulate these ratios: one, that the more important and serious the deliberations are, the closer the prevailing opinion should be to unanimity; the other, that the more the matter at hand calls for alacrity, the smaller the prescribed difference in the division of opinion should be. In decisions that must be reached immediately, a majority of a single vote should suffice. The first of these maxims seems more suited to the laws and the second to public business. Be that as it may, it is the combination of the two that establishes the ratios that best help the majority to render its decision.

QUESTIONS FOR THOUGHT/DISCUSSION:

➤ Rousseau indicates here a major danger in the formation of what we might call 'special interest groups' in society. What does he believe is the danger posed and what does he propose as a way of curbing the power or influence of such groups?

➤ Rousseau outlines a type of direct democracy or participatory democracy; the people maintain their sovereignty by making the decisions for the whole through voting and then designating a government entity to carry out the wishes of the body politic. What sort of problems might ensue in this type of governing system?

➤ What would happen in Rousseau's system if most of the votes of the body politic were passed by only a one-vote margin?

II. John Locke:
Second Treatise of Government

John Locke (1632 1704) was a British philosopher during the Enlightened Era. He was a philosopher, physician, teacher, statesman, economist, and counsel to kings. He was from a wealthy English family and was educated at Westminster and Oxford. Locke was most famous during his life for his Essay Concerning Human Understanding. His Two Treatises of Government were written to justify revolution against the monarchy in England, and succeeded in justifying revolutions in America and France, against monarchs, a century later. His political writings received more attention after his death than during his life. In fact, he denied being the author of the Two Treatises throughout his life.

John Locke's Second Treatise of Government is considered the best treatise ever written on Natural Rights Democracy. In it you will find many of the concepts that we have come to accept as absolutes: the social contract, natural rights, majority rule, consent of the governed, limited representative government, sovereignty of the people, the rule of law, the right of revolution, and the riddance of the divine right of kings. While today we might place some of our own founding fathers in that class of men known as the enlightened philosophers, they would have considered themselves merely followers of John Locke. Indeed, he had a profound impact on those who lived at the same time he did, as well as on everyone who followed him.

"We hold these truths to be self-evident, that all men are created equal, that they are endowed by their creator with certain unalienable rights, that among these are life, liberty, and the pursuit of happiness. That to secure these rights, governments are instituted among men, deriving their just powers from the consent of the governed. That whenever any form of government becomes destructive of these ends, it is the right of the people to alter or abolish it, and to institute new government." This passage from the Declaration of

Independence, written by Thomas Jefferson, embodies many of the principles of Locke's natural rights democracy.

The selected excerpts reprinted here were taken from Chapters 8, 9, and 11 of the Second Treatise.

John Locke: Second Treatise of Government

Of the Beginning of Political Societies

Men being, as has been said, by nature all free, equal, and independent, no one can be put out of this state and subjected to the political power of another without his own consent, which is done by agreeing with other men to join and unite into a community for their comfortable, safe, and peaceable living, one amongst another, in a secure enjoyment of their properties and a greater security against any that are not of it. This any number of men may do, because it injures not the freedom of the rest; they are left, as they were, in the liberty of the state of nature. When any number of men have so consented to make one community or government, they are thereby presently incorporated and make one body politic, wherein the majority have a right to act and conclude the rest.

For, when any number of men have, by the consent of every individual, made a community, they have thereby made that community one body, with a power to act as one body, which is only by the will and determination of the majority. For that which acts as a community, being only the consent of the individuals in it—and it being one body, must move one way—it is necessary the body should move that way whither the greater force carries it, which is the consent of the majority, or else it is impossible it should act or continue as one body, one community, which the consent of every individual that united into it agreed that it should; and so every one is bound by that consent to be concluded by the majority. And therefore we see that in assemblies empowered to act by positive laws where no number is set by that positive law which empowers them, the act of the majority passes for the act of the whole, and of course determines as having, by the law of nature and reason, the power of the whole.

And thus every man, by consenting with others to make one body politic under one government, puts himself under an obligation to every one of that society to submit to the determination of the majority, and to be concluded by it; or else this original compact, whereby he with others incorporates into one society, would signify nothing, and be no compact if he be left free and under no other ties than he was in before in the state of nature. For what appearance would there be of any compact? What new engagement if he were no farther tied by any decrees of the society than he himself thought fit and did actually consent to? This would be still as great a liberty as he himself had before his compact, or any one else in the state of nature who may submit himself and consent to any acts of it if he thinks fit...

Whosoever, therefore, out of a state of nature unite into a community, must be understood to give up all the power necessary to the ends for which they unite into society to the majority of the community, unless they expressly agreed in any number greater than the majority. And this is done by barely agreeing to unite into one political society, which is all the compact that is, or needs be, between the individuals that enter into or make up a commonwealth. And thus, that which begins and actually constitutes any political society is nothing but the consent of any number of freemen capable of majority, to unite and incorporate into such a society. And this is that, and that only, which did or could give beginning to any lawful government in the world.

To this I find two objections made: 1. That there are no instances to be found in story of a company of men, independent and equal one amongst another, that met together and in this way began and set up a government. 2. It is impossible of right that men should do so, because all men, being born under government, they are to submit to that and are not at liberty to begin a new one.

To the first there is this to answer: That it is not at all to be wondered that history gives us but a very little account of men that lived together in the state of nature. The inconveniencies of that condition, and the love and want of society, no sooner brought any number of them together, but they presently united and incorporated if they designed to continue together. And if we may not suppose men ever to have been in the state of nature, because we hear not much of them in such a state, we may as well suppose the armies...were never children, because we hear little of them till they were men and embodied in armies. Government is everywhere antecedent to records, and letters seldom come in amongst a people till a long continuation of civil society has, by other more necessary arts, provided for their safety, ease, and plenty. And then they begin to look after the history of their founders, and search into their origin when they have outlived the memory of it. For it is with commonwealths as with particular persons, they are commonly ignorant of their own births and infancies; and if they know anything of it, they are beholden for it to the accidental records that others have kept of it. And those that we have of the beginning of any polities in the world...are all either plain instances of such a beginning as I have mentioned, or at least have manifest footsteps of it.

He must show a strange inclination to deny evident matter of fact, when it agrees not with his hypothesis, who will not allow that the beginning of Rome and Venice were by the uniting together of several men, free and independent one of another, amongst whom there was no natural superiority or subjection... So that their political societies all began from a voluntary union, and the mutual agreement of men freely acting in the choice of their governors and forms of government. And I hope those who went away from Sparta...will be allowed to have been freemen independent one of another, and to have set up a government over themselves by their own consent.

Thus I have given several examples out of history of people, free and in the state of nature, that, being met together, incorporated and began a commonwealth...

But, to conclude: reason being plain on our side that men are naturally free; and the examples of history showing that the governments of the world, that were begun in peace, had their beginning laid on that foundation, and were made by the consent of the people; there can be little room for doubt, either where the right is, or what has been the opinion or practice of mankind about the first erecting of governments.

I will not deny that if we look back, as far as history will direct us, towards the origin of commonwealths, we shall

generally find them under the government and administration of one man. And I am also apt to believe that where a
family was numerous enough to subsist by itself, and
continued entire together without mixing with others, as it
often happens where there is much land and few people, the
government commonly began in the father. For the father
having, by the law of nature, the same power with every man
else to punish as he thought fit any offences against that law,
might thereby punish his transgressing children even when
they were men and out of their pupillage; and they were very
likely to submit to his punishment, and all join with him
against the offender in their turns, giving him thereby power
to execute his sentence against any transgression and so, in
effect, make him the lawmaker and governor over all that
remained in conjunction with his family. He was fittest to be
trusted; paternal affection secured their property and interest
under his care, and the custom of obeying him in their
childhood made it easier to submit to him rather than any
other. If, therefore, they must have one to rule them, as
government is hardly to be avoided amongst men that live
together, who so likely to be the man as he that was their
common father unless negligence, cruelty, or any other defect
of mind or body made him unfit for it? But...where several
families met and consented to continue together, it is not to be
doubted, but they used their natural freedom to set up him
whom they judged the ablest and most likely to rule well over
them.

Thus, though looking back as far as records give us any
account of peopling the world and the history of nations, we
commonly find the government to be in one hand, yet it
destroys not that which I affirm—that the beginning of politic
society depends upon the consent of the individuals to join
into and make one society, who, when they are thus
incorporated, might set up what form of government they
thought fit. But this having given occasion to men to mistake
and think that by nature government was monarchical and
belonged to the father, it may not be amiss here to consider
why people, in the beginning, generally pitched upon this
form which, though perhaps the father's pre-eminency might
in the first institution of some commonwealths give a rise to
and place in the beginning the power in one hand, yet it is

plain that the reason that continued the form of government in a single person was not any regard or respect to paternal authority, since all petty monarchies—that is, almost all monarchies near their original, have been commonly, at least upon occasion, elective.

First, then, in the beginning of things, the father's government of the childhood of those sprung from him, having accustomed them to the rule of one man and taught them that where it was exercised with care and skill, with affection and love to those under it, it was sufficient to procure and preserve for men all the political happiness they sought for in society, it was no wonder that they should pitch upon and naturally run into that form of government which, from their infancy, they had all been accustomed to, and which by experience, they had found both easy and safe. To which if we add, that monarchy being simple and most obvious to men, whom neither experience had instructed in forms of government, nor the ambition or insolence of empire had taught to beware of the encroachments of prerogative or the inconveniencies of absolute power...it was not at all strange that they should not much trouble themselves to think of methods of restraining any exorbitances of those to whom they had given the authority over them, and of balancing the power of government by placing several parts of it in different hands. They had neither felt the oppression of tyrannical dominion, nor did the fashion of the age...give them any reason to apprehend or provide against it.

Therefore, it is no wonder they put themselves into such a frame of government as was not only, as I said, most obvious and simple, but also best suited to their present state and condition, which stood more in need of defense against foreign invasions and injuries than of multiplicity of laws where there was but very little property, and wanted not variety of rulers and abundance of officers to direct and look after their execution where there were but few trespassers and few offenders. Since, then, those who liked one another so well as to join into society cannot but be supposed to have some acquaintance and friendship together and some trust one in another, they could not but have greater apprehensions of others than of one another; and, therefore, their first care and thought cannot but be supposed to be how to secure themselves against foreign force. It was natural for them to put themselves under a frame of government which might best serve to that end and choose the wisest and bravest man to conduct them in their wars and lead them out against their enemies, and in this chiefly be their ruler...

Thus, whether a family, by degrees, grew up into a commonwealth, and the fatherly authority being continued on to the elder son, every one in his turn growing up under it tacitly submitted to it, and the easiness and equality of it not offending any one, every one acquiesced till time seemed to have confirmed it and settled a right of succession by prescription; or whether several families or the descendants of several families, whom chance, neighborhood, or business brought together, united into society; the need of a general whose conduct might defend them against their enemies in war...made the first beginners of commonwealths generally put the rule into one man's hand, without any other express limitation or restraint but what the nature of the thing and the end of government required. It was given them for the public good and safety, and to those ends, in the infancies of commonwealths, they commonly used it; and unless they had done so, young societies could not have subsisted. Without such nursing fathers, without this care of the governors, all governments would have sunk under the weakness and infirmities of their infancy...

But the golden age...had more virtue, and consequently better governors as well as less vicious subjects; and there was then no stretching prerogative on the one side to oppress the people, nor, consequently, on the other, any dispute about privilege to lessen or restrain the power of the magistrate; and so no contest betwixt rulers and people about governors or government. Yet, when ambition and luxury in future ages would retain and increase the power, without doing the business for which it was given, and aided by flattery, taught princes to have distinct and separate interests from their people, men found it necessary to examine more carefully the origin and rights of government, and to find ways to restrain the exorbitances and prevent the abuses of that power, which they, having entrusted in another's hands only for their own good, found was made use of to hurt them.

Thus we may see how probable it is that people who were naturally free, and, by their own consent, either submitted to the government of their father or united together...to make a government, should generally put the rule into one man's hands, and choose to be under the conduct of a single person, without so much as, by express conditions, limiting or regulating his power, which they thought safe enough in his honesty and prudence; though they never dreamed of monarchy being jure Divino, which we never heard of among mankind till it was revealed to us by the divinity of this last age, nor ever allowed paternal power to have a right to dominion or to be the foundation of all government. And thus much may suffice to show that, as far as we have any light from history, we have reason to conclude that all peaceful beginnings of government have been laid in the consent of the people. I say "peaceful" because I shall have occasion in another place to speak of conquest, which some esteem a way of beginning governments.

The other objection, I find, urged against the beginning of polities, in the way I have mentioned, is this: "That all men being born under government, some or other, it is impossible any of them should ever be free and at liberty to unite together and begin a new one, or ever be able to erect a lawful government." If this argument be good, I ask: how came so many lawful monarchies into the world? For if anybody, upon this supposition, can show me any one man, in any age of the world, free to begin a lawful monarchy, I will be bound to show him ten other free men at liberty, at the same time, to unite and begin a new government under a regal or any other form. It being demonstrated that if any one born under the dominion of another may be so free as to have a right to command others in a new and distinct empire, every one that is born under the dominion of another may be so free too, and may become a ruler or subject of a distinct separate government. And so, by this their own principle, either all men, however born, are free, or else there is but one lawful prince, one lawful government in the world; and then they have nothing to do but barely to show us which that is, which, when they have done, I doubt not but all mankind will easily agree to pay obedience to him.

Though it be a sufficient answer to their objection to show that it involves them in the same difficulties that it doth those they use it against, yet I shall endeavor to discover the weakness of this argument a little farther. "All men," say they, "are born under government, and therefore they cannot be at liberty to begin a new one. Every one is born a subject to his father or his prince, and is therefore under the perpetual tie of subjection and allegiance." It is plain mankind never owned nor considered any such natural subjection that they were born in, to one or to the other, that tied them, without their own consents, to a subjection to them and their heirs...

But it is plain governments themselves understand it otherwise; they claim no power over the son because of that they had over the father; nor look on children as being their subjects, by their fathers being so. If a subject of England should have a child by an Englishwoman in France, whose subject is he? Not the King of England's, for he must have leave to be admitted to the privileges of it. Nor the King of France's, for how then has his father a liberty to bring him away, and breed him as he pleases; and whoever was judged as a traitor or deserter, if he left, or warred against a country, for being barely born in it of parents that were aliens there? It is plain, then, by the practice of governments themselves, as well as by the law of right reason, that a child is born a subject of no country nor government. He is under his father's tuition and authority till he comes to the age of discretion, and then he is a free man, at liberty as to what government he will put himself under, what body politic he will unite himself to...

Of the Ends of Political Society and Government

If man in the state of nature be so free as has been said, if he be absolute lord of his own person and possessions, equal to the greatest and subject to nobody, why will he part with his freedom, this empire, and subject himself to the dominion and control of any other power? To which it is obvious to answer, that though in the state of nature he hath such a right, yet the enjoyment of it is very uncertain and constantly exposed to the invasion of others; for all being kings as much as he, every man his equal, and the greater part no strict observers of equity and justice, the enjoyment of the property he has in this state is very unsafe, very insecure. This makes him willing to quit this condition which, however free, is full of fears and continual dangers; and it is not without reason that he seeks out and is willing to join in society with others who are already united, or have a mind to unite for the mutual preservation of their lives, liberties, and estates, which I call by the general name of property.

The great and chief end, therefore, of men uniting into commonwealths, and putting themselves under government, is the preservation of their property, to which in the state of nature there are many things wanting. Firstly, there wants an established, settled, known law, received and allowed by common consent to be the standard of right and wrong, and the common measure to decide all controversies between them. For though the law of nature be plain and intelligible to all rational creatures, yet men, being biased by their interest, as well as ignorant for want of study of it, are not apt to allow of it as a law binding to them in the application of it to their particular cases.

Secondly, in the state of nature there wants a known and indifferent judge, with authority to determine all differences according to the established law. For every one in that state being both judge and executioner of the law of nature, men being partial to themselves, passion and revenge is very apt to carry them too far...

Thirdly, in the state of nature there often wants power to back and support the sentence when right, and to give it due execution. They, who by any injustice offended, will seldom fail where they are able by force to make good their injustice. Such resistance many times makes the punishment danger-ous, and frequently destructive to those who attempt it.

Thus, mankind, notwithstanding all the privileges of the state of nature, being but in an ill condition while they remain in it, are quickly driven into society. Hence it comes to pass, that we seldom find any number of men live any time together in this state. The inconveniencies that they are therein exposed to by the irregular and uncertain exercise of the power every man has of punishing the transgressions of others, make them take sanctuary under the established laws of government, and therein seek the preservation of their property. It is this that makes them so willingly give up, every one, his single power of punishing to be exercised by such alone as shall be appointed to it amongst them, and by such rules as the community, or those authorized by them to that purpose, shall agree on. And in this we have the original right and rise of both the legislative and executive power, as well as of the governments and societies themselves.

For in the state of nature, to omit the liberty he has of innocent delights, a man has two powers. The first is to do whatsoever he thinks fit for the preservation of himself and others within the permission of the law of nature... The other power a man has in the state of nature is the power to punish the crimes committed against that law. Both these he gives up when he joins in a private...or particular political society, and incorporates into any commonwealth separate from the rest of mankind.

The first power...of doing whatsoever he thought fit for the preservation of himself and the rest of mankind, he gives up to be regulated by laws made by the society, so far forth as the preservation of himself and the rest of that society shall require, which laws of the society in many things confine the liberty he had by the law of Nature.

Secondly, the power of punishing he wholly gives up, and engages his natural force, which he might before employ in the execution of the law of nature by his own single authority as he thought fit, to assist the executive power of the society as the law thereof shall require. For being now in a new state, wherein he is to enjoy many conveniences from the labor, assistance, and society of others in the same community, as well as protection from its whole strength, he is to part also with as much of his natural liberty, in providing for himself, as the good, prosperity, and safety of the society shall require, which is not only necessary but just, since the other members of the society do the like.

But though men, when they enter into society, give up the equality, liberty, and executive power they had in the state of nature into the hands of the society, to be so far disposed of by the legislative as the good of the society shall require, yet it being only with an intention in every one the better to preserve himself, his liberty and property...the power of the society or legislative constituted by them can never be supposed to extend farther than the common good, but is obliged to secure every one's property by providing against those three defects above mentioned that made the state of nature so unsafe and uneasy. And so, whoever has the legislative or supreme power of any commonwealth, is bound to govern by established standing laws, promulgated and known to the people, and not by extemporary decrees, by indifferent and upright judges, who are to decide controversies by those laws; and to employ the force of the community at home only in the execution of such laws, or abroad to prevent or redress foreign injuries and secure the community from inroads and invasion—and all this to be directed to no other end but the peace, safety, and public good of the people.

Of the Extent of the Legislative Power

The great end of men's entering into society being the enjoyment of their properties in peace and safety, and the great instrument and means of that being the laws established in that society, the first and fundamental positive law of all commonwealths is the establishing of the legislative power, as the first and fundamental natural law which is to govern even the legislative. Itself is the preservation of the society and (as far as will consist with the public good) of every person in it. This legislative is not only the supreme power of the commonwealth, but sacred and unalterable in the hands where the community have once placed it. Nor can any edict of anybody else, in what form so ever conceived, or by what power so ever backed, have the force and obligation of a law which has not its sanction from that legislative which the public has chosen and appointed; for without this the law could not have that which is absolutely necessary to its being a law, the consent of the society, over whom nobody can have a power to make laws but by their own consent and by authority received from them; and therefore all the obedience, which by the most solemn ties any one can be obliged to pay, ultimately terminates in this supreme power, and is directed by those laws which it enacts. Nor can any oaths to any foreign power whatsoever, or any domestic subordinate power, discharge any member of the society from his obedience to the legislative, acting pursuant to their trust, nor oblige him to any obedience contrary to the laws so enacted or farther than they do allow, it being ridiculous to imagine one can be tied ultimately to obey any power in the society which is not the supreme.

Though the legislative, whether placed in one or more, whether it be always in being or only by intervals, though it be the supreme power in every commonwealth...it is not, nor can possibly be, absolutely arbitrary over the lives and fortunes of the people. For it being but the joint power of every member of the society given up to that person or assembly which is legislator, it can be no more than those persons had in a state of nature before they entered into society, and gave it up to the community. For nobody can transfer to another more power than he has in himself, and nobody has an absolute arbitrary power over himself, or over any other, to destroy his own life, or take away the life or property of another. A man, as has been proved, cannot subject himself to the arbitrary power of another; and having, in the state of nature, no arbitrary power over the life, liberty, or possession of another, but only so much as the law of nature gave him for the preservation of himself and the rest of mankind, this is all he doth, or can give up to the commonwealth, and by it to the legislative power, so that the legislative can have no more than this.

Their power in the utmost bounds of it is limited to the public good of the society. It is a power that hath no other end but preservation, and therefore can never have a right to destroy, enslave, or designedly to impoverish the subjects. The obligations of the law of nature cease not in society, but only in many cases are drawn closer, and have, by human laws, known penalties annexed to them to enforce their observation. Thus the law of nature stands as an eternal rule to all men, legislators as well as others. The rules that they make for other men's actions must, as well as their own and other men's actions, be conformable to the law of nature...of which that is a declaration, and the fundamental law of nature being the preservation of mankind, no human sanction can be good or valid against it.

Secondly, the legislative or supreme authority cannot assume to itself a power to rule by extemporary arbitrary decrees, but is bound to dispense justice and decide the rights of the subject by promulgated standing laws, and known authorized judges. For the law of nature being unwritten, and so nowhere to be found but in the minds of men, they who, through passion or interest, shall...misapply it, cannot so easily be convinced of their mistake where there is no established judge; and so it serves not as it ought, to determine the rights and fence the properties of those that live under it, especially where every one is judge, interpreter, and executioner of it too, and that in his own case; and he that has right on his side, having ordinarily but his own single strength, hath not force enough to defend himself from injuries or punish delinquents. To avoid these inconveniences, which disorder men's properties in the state of nature, men unite into societies that they may have the united strength of the whole society to secure and defend their properties, and may have standing rules to bound it by which every one may know what is his. To this end it is that men give up all their natural power to the society they enter into, and the community put the legislative power into such hands as they think fit with this trust, that they shall be governed by declared laws, or else their peace, quiet, and property will still be at the same uncertainty as it was in the state of nature.

Absolute arbitrary power, or governing without settled standing laws, can neither of them consist with the ends of society and government, which men would not quit the freedom of the state of nature for, and tie themselves up under, were it not to preserve their lives, liberties, and fortunes, and by stated rules of right and property to secure their peace and quiet. It cannot be supposed that they should intend, had they a power so to do, to give any one or more an absolute arbitrary power over their persons and estates, and put a force into the magistrate's hand to execute his unlimited will arbitrarily upon them; this were to put themselves into a worse condition than the state of nature, wherein they had a liberty to defend their right against the injuries of others, and were upon equal terms of force to maintain it, whether invaded by a single man or many in combination... And, therefore, whatever form the commonwealth is under, the ruling power ought to govern by declared and received laws, and not by extempory dictates and undetermined resolutions, for then mankind will be in a far worse condition than in the state of nature if they shall have armed one or a few men with the joint power of a multitude, to force them to obey at pleasure the exorbitant and unlimited decrees of their sudden thoughts...without having any measures set down which may guide and justify their actions. For all the power the government has, being only for the good of the society, as it ought not to be arbitrary and at pleasure, so it ought to be exercised by established and promulgated laws, that both the people may know their duty, and be safe and secure within the limits of the law, and the rulers, too, kept within their due bounds, and not be tempted by the power they have in their hands to employ it to purposes, and by such measures as they would not have known, and own not willingly.

Thirdly, the supreme power cannot take from any man any part of his property without his own consent. For the preservation of property being the end of government, and that for which men enter into society, it necessarily supposes and requires that the people should have property, without which they must be supposed to lose that by entering into society which was the end for which they entered into it; too gross an absurdity for any man to own. Men, therefore, in society having property, they have such a right to the goods, which by the law of the community are theirs, that nobody hath a right to take them, or any part of them, from them without their own consent; without this they have no property at all. For I have truly no property in that which another can by right take from me when he pleases against my consent. Hence it is a mistake to think that the supreme or legislative power of any commonwealth can do what it will, and dispose of the estates of the subject arbitrarily, or take any part of them at pleasure... For a man's property is not at all secure, though there be good and equitable laws to set the bounds of it between him and his fellow subjects, if he who commands those subjects have power to take from any private man what part he pleases of his property, and use and dispose of it as he thinks good...

It is true governments cannot be supported without great charge, and it is fit every one who enjoys his share of the protection should pay out of his estate his proportion for the maintenance of it. But still it must be with his own consent...the consent of the majority, giving it either by themselves or their representatives chosen by them; for if any one shall claim a power to lay and levy taxes on the people by his own authority, and without such consent of the people, he thereby invades the fundamental law of property, and subverts the end of government. For what property have I in that which another may by right take when he pleases to himself?

Fourthly, the legislative cannot transfer the power of making laws to any other hands, for it being but a delegated power from the people, they who have it cannot pass it over to others. The people alone can appoint the form of the commonwealth, which is by constituting the legislative, and appointing in whose hands that shall be. And when the people have said, "We will submit, and be governed by laws made by such men, and in such forms," nobody else can say other men shall make laws for them; nor can they be bound by any laws but such as are enacted by those whom they have chosen and authorized to make laws for them.

These are the bounds which the trust that is put in them by the society and the law of God and nature have set to the legislative power of every commonwealth, in all forms of government. First: They are to govern by promulgated established laws, not to be varied in particular cases, but to have one rule for rich and poor, for the favorite at court, and the countryman at plough. Secondly: These laws also ought to be designed for no other end ultimately but the good of the people. Thirdly: They must not raise taxes on the property of the people without the consent of the people given by themselves or their deputies. And this properly concerns only such governments where the legislative is always in being, or at least where the people have not reserved any part of the legislative to deputies, to be from time to time chosen by themselves. Fourthly: Legislative neither must nor can transfer the power of making laws to anybody else, or place it anywhere but where the people have.

QUESTIONS FOR THOUGHT/DISCUSSION:

- ➤ John Locke addresses the argument from those who say that we have no way of knowing how or why governments were originally formed. What does he say about this?
- ➤ Do you think Locke considered "the rule of law" to be a good thing?
- ➤ Read Amendment 14, Section 1 of the U.S. Constitution. Do you find anything in the reading here from John Locke about due process and the equal protection of the laws?

III. James Madison:
Federalist Paper #10

James Madison (1751-1836) began his national political career as a delegate from Virginia at the Continental Congress in 1776. This career culminated in his being elected to two terms as our third president (1809-1817). In between he served as one of Virginia's representatives in the House of Representatives, and as Thomas Jefferson's Secretary of State.

He is also considered the author of the Bill of Rights. But, while he did author the final version, he was completely against the concept. (Patrick Henry should, more properly, be considered the originator. It was his persistence, as one of the anti-federalists, which finally culminated in the addition.) Madison was worried about two things concerning the Bill of Rights: first, that all individual liberties were already guaranteed simply by not being denied. And, second, that a list of liberties could never be all-inclusive and might have the future result of a loss of those liberties not listed. In authoring the Bill of Rights, Madison addressed his two concerns with the Ninth and Tenth Amendments.

Posterity remembers James Madison best as the Father of the United States Constitution, not because he wrote the document in its entirety by himself, but because the draft he brought with him to the Constitutional Convention in Philadelphia in 1787 bears a striking resemblance to the final product. He was by far the most influential delegate present who took the most comprehensive notes, and it was he who put the words and ideas of the many delegates into the final prose. It was also he, along with Alexander Hamilton and John Jay, who defended the Constitution during the ratification process through a series of essays published in the New York newspapers explaining the new Constitution and expressing the reasons for accepting it. These essays are known to us, collectively, as The Federalist Papers.

Printed here is the most famous of all the essays. Federalist Paper #10 has always been thought of as Madison's

Good

dissertation on the reasons why 'factions' are a necessary evil that we must seek to control. These 'factions,' in our parlance, can be thought of as political parties or special interest groups. Madison was concerned that these smaller groups in society would seek to control the political agenda and we would find ourselves with a tyranny of the minority.

Federalist #10 has value, though, much beyond Madison's views on the evils of factions. In attempting to show us how to control these factions without compromising the people's liberties, Madison outlines the entire system of government that has just been created and illustrates all of the reasons why this government is the best possible system. As you read this essay look for Madison's explanation of constitutional democracy, the federal system of government, the separation of powers, checks and balances, and representative government. Also, look for his views on representatives themselves, and how they should behave while in office, and the relationship between national and state government. This is the Federalist Paper that illustrates the true genius of James Madison.

James Madison: Federalist Paper #10

Among the numerous advantages promised by a well-constructed Union, none deserves to be more accurately developed than its tendency to break and control the violence of faction. The friend of popular governments never finds himself so much alarmed for their character and fate, as when he contemplates their propensity to this dangerous vice. He will not fail, therefore, to set a due value on any plan, which without violating the principles to which he is attached provides a proper cure for it. The instability, injustice, and confusion introduced into the public councils, have, in truth, been the mortal diseases under which popular governments have everywhere perished, as they continue to be the favorite and fruitful topics from which the adversaries to liberty derive their most specious declamations.

The valuable improvements made by the American constitutions on the popular models, both ancient and modern, cannot certainly be too much admired; but it would be an unwarrantable partiality, to contend that they have as effectually obviated the danger on this side, as was wished and expected. Complaints are everywhere heard from our most considerate and virtuous citizens, equally the friends of public and private faith, and of public and personal liberty, that our governments are too unstable, that the public good is disregarded in the conflicts of rival parties, and that measures are too often decided, not according to the rules of justice and the rights of the minor party, but by the superior force of an interested and overbearing majority. However anxiously we may wish that these complaints had no foundation, the evidence of known facts will not permit us to deny that they are in some degree true.

It will be found, indeed, on a candid review of our situation, that some of the distresses under which we labor have been erroneously charged on the operation of our governments; but it will be found, at the same time, that other causes will not alone account for many of our heaviest misfortunes; and, particularly, for that prevailing and increasing distrust of public engagements, and alarm for private rights, which are echoed from one end of the continent to the other. These must be chiefly, if not wholly, effects of the unsteadiness and injustice with which a factious spirit has tainted our public administrations. By a faction, I understand a number of citizens, whether amounting to a majority or a minority of the whole, who are united and actuated by some common impulse of passion, or of interest, adverse to the rights of other citizens, or to the permanent and aggregate interests of the community.

There are two methods of curing the mischiefs of faction: the one, by removing its causes, the other, by controlling its effects. There are again two methods of removing the causes of faction: the one, by destroying the liberty which is essential to its existence; the other, by giving to every citizen the same opinions, the same passions, and the same interests. It could never be more truly said than of the first remedy, that it was worse than the disease. Liberty is to faction what air is to fire, an aliment without which it instantly expires. But it could not be less folly to abolish liberty, which is essential to political life, because it nourishes faction, than it would be to wish the annihilation of air, which is essential to animal life, because it imparts to fire its destructive agency.

The second expedient is as impracticable as the first would be unwise. As long as the reason of man continues fallible, and he is at liberty to exercise it, different opinions will be formed. As long as the connection subsists between his reason and his self-love, his opinions and his passions will have a reciprocal influence on each other; and the former will be objects to which the latter will attach themselves.

The diversity in the faculties of men, from which the rights of property originate, is not less an insuperable obstacle to a uniformity of interests. The protection of these faculties is the first object of government. From the protection of different and unequal faculties of acquiring property, the possession of different degrees and kinds of property immediately results; and from the influence of these on the sentiments and views of the respective proprietors, ensues a division of the society into different interests and parties.

The latent causes of faction are thus sown in the nature of man; and we see them everywhere brought into different degrees of activity, according to the different circumstances of civil society. A zeal for different opinions concerning religion, concerning government, and many other points, as well of speculation as of practice; an attachment to different leaders ambitiously contending for pre-eminence and power; or to persons of other descriptions whose fortunes have been interesting to the human passions, have, in turn, divided mankind into parties, inflamed them with mutual animosity, and rendered them much more disposed to vex and oppress each other than to cooperate for their common good. So strong is this propensity of mankind to fall into mutual animosities, that where no substantial occasion presents itself, the most frivolous and fanciful distinctions have been sufficient to kindle their unfriendly passions and excite their most violent conflicts.

But the most common and durable source of factions has been the various and unequal distribution of property. Those who hold and those who are without property have ever formed distinct interests in society. Those who are creditors, and those who are debtors, fall under a like discrimination. A landed interest, a manufacturing interest, a mercantile interest, a moneyed interest, with many lesser interests, grow up of necessity in civilized nations, and divide them into different classes, actuated by different sentiments and views.

The regulation of these various and interfering interests forms the principal task of modern legislation, and involves the spirit of party and faction in the necessary and ordinary operations of the government. No man is allowed to be a judge in his own cause, because his interest would certainly bias his judgment, and, not improbably, corrupt his integrity. With equal, nay with greater reason, a body of men are unfit to be both judges and parties at the same time; yet what are many of the most important acts of legislation, but so many judicial determinations, not indeed concerning the rights of single persons, but concerning the rights of large bodies of citizens? And what are the different classes of legislators but advocates and parties to the causes which they determine? Is a law proposed concerning private debts? It is a question to which the creditors are parties on one side and the debtors on the other. Justice ought to hold the balance between them. Yet the parties are, and must be, themselves the judges; and the most numerous party, or, in other words, the most powerful faction must be expected to prevail. Shall domestic manufactures be encouraged, and in what degree, by restrictions on foreign manufactures? These are questions which would be differently decided by the landed and the manufacturing classes, and probably by neither with a sole regard to justice and the public good.

The apportionment of taxes on the various descriptions of property is an act which seems to require the most exact impartiality; yet there is, perhaps, no legislative act in which greater opportunity and temptation are given to a predominant party to trample on the rules of justice. Every shilling with which they overburden the inferior number, is a shilling saved to their own pockets.

It is in vain to say that enlightened statesmen will be able to adjust these clashing interests, and render them all subservient to the public good. Enlightened statesmen will not always be at the helm. Nor, in many cases, can such an adjustment be made at all without taking into view indirect and remote considerations, which will rarely prevail over the immediate interest which one party may find in disregarding the rights of another or the good of the whole.

The inference to which we are brought is, that the causes of faction cannot be removed, and that relief is only to be sought in the means of controlling its effects. If a faction consists of less than a majority, relief is supplied by the republican principle, which enables the majority to defeat its sinister views by regular vote. It may clog the administration, it may convulse the society; but it will be unable to execute and mask its violence under the forms of the Constitution. When a majority is included in a faction, the form of popular government, on the other hand, enables it to sacrifice to its ruling passion or interest both the public good and the rights of other citizens. To secure the public good and private rights against the danger of such a faction, and at the same time to preserve the spirit and the form of popular government, is then the great object to which our inquiries are directed.

Let me add that it is the great desideratum by which this form of government can be rescued from the opprobrium under which it has so long labored, and be recommended to the esteem and adoption of mankind. By what means is this object attainable? Evidently by one of two only. Either the existence of the same passion or interest in a majority at the same time must be prevented, or the majority, having such coexistent passion or interest, must be rendered, by their number and local situation, unable to concert and carry into effect schemes of oppression. If the impulse and the opportunity be suffered to coincide, we well know that neither moral nor religious motives can be relied on as an adequate control. They are not found to be such on the injustice and violence of individuals, and lose their efficacy in proportion to the number combined together, that is, in proportion as their efficacy becomes needful.

From this view of the subject it may be concluded that a pure democracy, by which I mean a society consisting of a small number of citizens, who assemble and administer the government in person, can admit of no cure for the mischiefs of faction. A common passion or interest will, in almost every case, be felt by a majority of the whole; a communication and concert result from the form of government itself; and there is nothing to check the inducements to sacrifice the weaker party or an obnoxious individual. Hence it is that such democracies have ever been spectacles of turbulence and contention; have ever been found incompatible with personal security or the rights of property; and have in general been as short in their lives as they have been violent in their deaths.

Theoretic politicians, who have patronized this species of government, have erroneously supposed that by reducing mankind to a perfect equality in their political rights, they would, at the same time, be perfectly equalized and assimilated in their possessions, their opinions, and their passions. A republic, by which I mean a government in which the scheme of representation takes place, opens a different prospect, and promises the cure for which we are seeking.

Let us examine the points in which it varies from pure democracy, and we shall comprehend both the nature of the cure and the efficacy, which it must derive from the Union. The two great points of difference between a democracy and a republic are: first, the delegation of the government, in the latter, to a small number of citizens elected by the rest; secondly, the greater number of citizens, and greater sphere of country, over which the latter may be extended. The effect of the first difference is, on the one hand, to refine and enlarge the public views, by passing them through the medium of a chosen body of citizens, whose wisdom may best discern the true interest of their country, and whose patriotism and love of justice will be least likely to sacrifice it to temporary or partial considerations. Under such a regulation, it may well happen that the public voice, pronounced by the representatives of the people, will be more consonant to the public good than if pronounced by the people themselves, convened for the purpose. On the other hand, the effect may be inverted. Men of factious tempers, of local prejudices, or of sinister designs, may, by intrigue, by corruption, or by other means, first obtain the suffrages, and then betray the interests, of the people.

The question resulting is, whether small or extensive republics are more favorable to the election of proper guardians of the public weal; and it is clearly decided in favor of the latter by two obvious considerations: In the first place, it is to be remarked that, however small the republic may be, the representatives must be raised to a certain number, in order to guard against the cabals of a few; and that, however large it may be, they must be limited to a certain number, in order to guard against the confusion of a multitude. Hence, the number of representatives in the two cases not being in proportion to that of the two constituents, and being proportionally greater in the small republic, it follows that, if the proportion of fit characters be not less in the large than in the small republic, the former will present a greater option, and consequently a greater probability of a fit choice.

In the next place, as each representative will be chosen by a greater number of citizens in the large than in the small republic, it will be more difficult for unworthy candidates to practice with success the vicious arts by which elections are too often carried; and the suffrages of the people being more free, will be more likely to center in men who possess the most attractive merit and the most diffusive and established characters. It must be confessed that in this, as in most other cases, there is a mean, on both sides of which inconveniences will be found to lie. By enlarging too much the number of electors, you render the representatives too little acquainted with all their local circumstances and lesser interests; as by reducing it too much, you render him unduly attached to these, and too little fit to comprehend and pursue great and national objects.

The federal Constitution forms a happy combination in this respect: the great and aggregate interests being referred to the national, the local and particular to the State legislatures. The other point of difference is, the greater number of citizens and extent of territory which may be brought within the compass of republican than of democratic government; and it is this circumstance principally which renders factious combinations less to be dreaded in the former than in the latter. The smaller the society, the fewer probably will be the distinct parties and interests composing it; the fewer the distinct parties and interests, the more frequently will a majority be found of the same party; and the smaller the number of individuals composing a majority, and the smaller the compass within which they are placed, the more easily will they concert and execute their plans of oppression. Extend the sphere, and you take in a greater variety of parties and interests; you make it less probable that a majority of the whole will have a common motive to invade the rights of other citizens; or if such a common motive exists, it will be more difficult for all who feel it to discover their own strength, and to act in unison with each other. Besides other impediments, it may be remarked that, where there is a consciousness of unjust or dishonorable purposes, communication is always checked by distrust in proportion to the number whose concurrence is necessary.

Hence, it clearly appears, that the same advantage which a republic has over a democracy, in controlling the effects of faction, is enjoyed by a large over a small republic, is enjoyed by the Union over the States composing it. Does the advantage consist in the substitution of representatives whose enlightened views and virtuous sentiments render them superior to local prejudices and schemes of injustice? It will not be denied that the representation of the Union will be most likely to possess these requisite endowments. Does it consist in the greater security afforded by a greater variety of parties, against the event of any one party being able to outnumber and oppress the rest? In an equal degree does the increased variety of parties comprised within the Union, increase this security. Does it, in fine, consist in the greater obstacles opposed to the concert and accomplishment of the secret wishes of an unjust and interested majority? Here, again, the extent of the Union gives it the most palpable advantage. The influence of factious leaders may kindle a flame within their particular States, but will be unable to spread a general conflagration through the other States. A religious sect may degenerate into a political faction in a part of the Confederacy; but the variety of sects dispersed over the entire face of it must secure the national councils against any danger from that source. A rage for paper money, for an abolition of debts, for an equal division of property, or for any other improper or wicked project, will be less apt to pervade the whole body of the Union than a particular member of it; in the same proportion as such a malady is more likely to taint a particular county or district, than an entire State.

In the extent and proper structure of the Union, therefore, we behold a republican remedy for the diseases most incident to republican government. And according to the degree of pleasure and pride we feel in being republicans, ought to be our zeal in cherishing the spirit and supporting the character of Federalists.

QUESTIONS FOR THOUGHT / DISCUSSION:

➤ While Madison spends a considerable amount of time here on the dangers of 'factions,' he also outlines the type of government structure created in this new republic. What does he believe is the significance of the federal system of government created by this new constitution?

➤ Elected representatives can be delegates or trustees—that is, they can vote their constituency or their conscience. Which does Madison believe is best?

➤ What are Madison's views on democracy? How do his ideas on the topics in the previous two questions explain his philosophy on securing the greatest good for the greatest number?

IV. Alexis de Toqueville:
Democracy in America

Alexis de Toqueville (1805-1859) was a French statesman, philosopher, and writer who traveled to America in the early 1830s to observe the young republic. He found many of our ways fascinating, including our level of energy and tendency of all members of society to engage in political debate. When he finished touring America he returned to France and wrote the classic 'Democracy in America.'

In 'Democracy in America' there are numerous criticisms of America's brand of democracy. It must be remembered, however, that Toqueville was not attempting to write a glowing endorsement of America and its democratic system. He was analyzing our system to see what was good and what was bad, what worked well, what didn't work at all, and what would work with a few adjustments. One must also keep in mind that Toqueville was a young boy during the French Revolution and was very directly touched by the excesses of majoritarianism. He was a member of the aristocracy—many of whom lost their heads on the guillotine. Toqueville was very much aware that while democracy might procure the greatest good for the greatest number, democracy also has the potential to grow into a tyranny if the rights of the minority are not safeguarded.

The following selection is taken from Toqueville's Democracy in America, which should be required reading in all high schools, for its prophetic value if nothing else. His insight about America's present (at that time) and future was phenomenal.

As you read this selection, pay particular attention to the way Toqueville looks at American patriotism as a sort of outgrowth of democracy—or is democracy an outgrowth of patriotism? He also discusses the 'rule of law' that he sees operating in this American democracy. He observes that the rule of law operates because we are a democracy; the people make the law and are therefore more willing to abide by it and see that their fellow citizens abide by it. The rule of law also allows us to pursue our own happiness secure in the knowledge that the law is there to protect our livelihood.

Alexis de Toqueville: Democracy in America

General Tendency of the Laws Under Democracy

The defects and weaknesses of a democratic government may readily be discovered; they can be proved by obvious facts, whereas their healthy influence becomes evident in ways which are not obvious and are, so to speak, hidden. A glance suffices to detect its faults, but its good qualities can be discerned only by long observation. The laws of the American democracy are frequently defective or incomplete; they sometimes attack vested rights, or sanction others which are dangerous to the community; and even if they were good, their frequency would still be a great evil. How comes it, then, that the American republics prosper and continue?

In the consideration of laws a distinction must be carefully observed between the end at which they aim and the means by which they pursue that end, between their absolute and their relative excellence. If it be the intention of the legislator to favor the interests of the minority at the expense of the majority, and if the measures he takes are so combined as to accomplish the object he has in view with the least possible expense of time and exertion, the law may be well drawn up although its purpose is bad; and the more efficacious it is, the more dangerous it will be.

Democratic laws generally tend to promote the welfare of the greatest possible number; for they emanate from the majority of the citizens, who are subject to error, but who cannot have an interest opposed to their own advantage. The laws of an aristocracy tend, on the contrary, to concentrate wealth and power in the hands of the minority because an aristocracy, by its very nature, constitutes a minority. It may therefore be asserted, as a general proposition, that the purpose of a democracy in its legislation is more useful to humanity than that of an aristocracy. This, however, is the sum total of its advantages. Aristocracies are infinitely more expert in the science of legislation than democracies ever can be. They are possessed of a self-control that protects them from the errors of temporary excitement; and they form far-reaching designs, which they know how to mature till a favorable opportunity arrives. Aristocratic government proceeds with the dexterity of art; it understands how to make the collective force of all its laws converge at the same time to a given point. Such is not the case with democracies, whose laws are almost always ineffective or inopportune. The means of democracy are therefore more imperfect than those of aristocracy, and the measures that it unwittingly adopts are frequently opposed to its own cause; but the object it has in view is more useful.

Let us now imagine a community so organized by nature or by its constitution that it can support the transitory action of bad laws, and that it can await, without destruction, the general tendency of its legislation: we shall then conceive how a democratic government, notwithstanding its faults, may be best fitted to produce the prosperity of this community. This is precisely what has occurred in the United States; and I repeat, what I have before remarked, that the great advantage of the Americans consists in their being able to commit faults which they may afterwards repair.

An analogous observation may be made respecting public officers. It is easy to perceive that American democracy frequently errs in the choice of the individuals to whom it entrusts the power of the administration; but it is more difficult to say why the state prospers under their rule. In the first place, it is to be remarked that if, in a democratic state, the governors have less honesty and less capacity than elsewhere, the governed are more enlightened and more attentive to their interests. As the people in democracies are more constantly vigilant in their affairs and more jealous of their rights, they prevent their representatives from abandoning that general line of conduct which their own interest prescribes. In the second place, it must be remembered that if the democratic magistrate is more apt to misuse his power, he possesses it for a shorter time. But there is yet another reason which is still more general and conclusive. It is no doubt of importance to the welfare of nations that they should be governed by men of talents and virtue; but it is perhaps still more important for them that the interests of those men should not differ from the interests of the community at large; for if such were the case, their virtues might become almost useless and their talents might be turned to a bad account. I have said that it is important that the interests of the persons in authority should not differ from or oppose the interests of the community at large; but I do not insist upon their having the same interests as the whole population, because I am not aware that such a state of things ever existed in any country.

No political form has hitherto been discovered that is equally favorable to the prosperity and the development of all the classes into which society is divided. These classes continue to form, as it were, so many distinct communities in the same nation; and experience has shown that it is no less dangerous to place the fate of these classes exclusively in the hands of any one of them than it is to make one people the arbiter of the destiny of another. When the rich alone govern, the interest of the poor is always endangered, and when the poor make the laws, that of the rich incurs very serious risks. The advantage of democracy does not consist, therefore, as has sometimes been asserted, in favoring the prosperity of all, but simply in contributing to the well being of the greatest number.

The men who are entrusted with the direction of public affairs in the United States are frequently inferior, in both capacity and morality, to those whom an aristocracy would raise to power. But their interest is identified and mingled with that of the majority of their fellow citizens. They may frequently be faithless and frequently mistaken, but they will never systematically adopt a line of conduct hostile to the majority; and they cannot give a dangerous or exclusive tendency to the government. The mal-administration of a democratic magistrate, moreover, is an isolated fact, which has influence only during the short period for which he is elected. Corruption and incapacity do not act as common interests which may connect men permanently with one another. A corrupt or incapable magistrate will not combine his measures with another magistrate simply because the latter is as corrupt and incapable as himself; and these two men will never unite their endeavors to promote the corruption and inaptitude of their remote posterity. The ambition and the maneuvers of the one will serve, on the contrary, to unmask the other. The vices of a magistrate in democratic states are usually wholly personal.

But under aristocratic governments public men are swayed by the interest of their order, which, if it is sometimes confused with the interests of the majority, is very frequently distinct from them. This interest is the common and lasting bond that unites them; it induces them to coalesce and combine their efforts to attain an end which is not always the happiness of the greatest number; and it serves not only to connect the persons in authority with one another, but to unite them with a considerable portion of the community, since a numerous body of citizens belong to the aristocracy without being invested with official functions. The aristocratic magistrate is therefore constantly supported by a portion of the community as well as by the government of which he is a member.

The common purpose, which in aristocracies connects the interest of the magistrates with that of a portion of their contemporaries, identifies it also with that of future generations; they labor for the future as well as for the present. The aristocratic magistrate is urged at the same time towards the same point by the passions of the community, by his own and, I may almost add, by those of his posterity. Is it, then, wonderful that he does not resist such repeated impulses? And, indeed, aristocracies are often carried away by their class spirit without being corrupted by it; and they unconsciously fashion society to their own ends and prepare it for their own descendants.

The English aristocracy is perhaps the most liberal that has ever existed, and no body of men has ever, uninterruptedly, furnished so many honorable and enlightened individuals to the government of a country. It cannot escape observation, however, that in the legislation of England the interests of the poor have often been sacrificed to the advantages of the rich, and the rights of the majority to the privileges of a few. The result is that England at the present day combines the extremes of good and evil fortune in the bosom of her society; and the miseries and privations of her poor almost equal her power and renown.

In the United States, where public officers have no class interests to promote, the general and constant influence of the government is beneficial, although the individuals who conduct it are frequently unskillful and sometimes contemptible. There is, indeed, a secret tendency in democratic institutions that makes the exertions of the citizens subservient to the prosperity of the community in spite of their vices and mistakes; while in aristocratic institutions there is a secret bias which, notwithstanding the talents and virtues of those who conduct the government, leads them to contribute to the evils that oppress their fellow creatures. In aristocratic governments public men may frequently do harm without intending it; and in democratic states they bring about good results of which they have never thought.

Public Spirit in the United States

There is one sort of patriotic attachment, which principally arises from that instinctive, disinterested, and indefinable feeling which connects the affections of man with his birthplace. This natural fondness is united with a taste for ancient customs and a reverence for traditions of the past; those who cherish it love their country as they love the mansion of their fathers. They love the tranquility that it affords them; they cling to the peaceful habits that they have contracted within its bosom; they are attached to the reminiscences that it awakens; and they are even pleased by living there in a state of obedience. This patriotism is sometimes stimulated by religious enthusiasm, and then it is capable of making prodigious efforts. It is in itself a kind of religion: it does not reason, but it acts from the impulse of faith and sentiment. In some nations the monarch is regarded as a personification of the country; and, the fervor of patriotism being converted into the fervor of loyalty, they take a sympathetic pride in his conquests, and glory in his power. Power was a time under the ancient monarchy when the French felt a sort of satisfaction in the sense of their dependence upon the arbitrary will of their king; and they were wont to say with pride: "We live under the most powerful king in the world."

But, like all instinctive passions, this kind of patriotism incites great transient exertions, but no continuity of effort. It may save the state in critical circumstances, but often allows it to decline in times of peace. While the manners of a people are simple and its faith unshaken, while society is steadily based upon traditional institutions whose legitimacy has never been contested, this instinctive patriotism is wont to endure. But there is another species of attachment to country, which is more rational than the one I have been describing. It is perhaps less generous and less ardent, but it is more fruitful and more lasting: it springs from knowledge, it is nurtured by the laws, it grows by the exercise of civil rights, and in the end it is confounded with the personal interests of the citizen. A man comprehends the influence which the well-being of his country has upon his own; he is aware that the laws permit him to contribute to that prosperity, and he labors to promote it, first because it benefits him, and secondly because it is in part his own work.

But epochs sometimes occur in the life of a nation when the old customs of a people are changed, public morality is destroyed, religious belief shaken, and the spell of tradition broken, while the diffusion of knowledge is yet imperfect and the civil rights of the community are ill secured or confined within narrow limits. The country then assumes a dim and dubious shape in the eyes of the citizens; they no longer behold it in the soil which they inhabit, for that soil is to them an inanimate clod; nor in the usages of their forefathers, which they have learned to regard as a debasing yoke; nor in religion, for of that they doubt; nor in the laws, which do not originate in their own authority; nor in the legislator, whom they fear and despise. The country is lost to their senses; they can discover it neither under its own nor under borrowed features and they retire into a narrow and unenlightened selfishness. They are emancipated from prejudice without having acknowledged the empire of reason; they have neither the instinctive patriotism of a monarchy nor the reflecting patriotism of a republic; but they have stopped between the two in the midst of confusion and distress.

In this predicament to retreat is impossible, for a people cannot recover the sentiments of their youth any more than a man can return to the innocent tastes of childhood; such things may be regretted, but they cannot be renewed. They must go forward and accelerate the union of private with public interests, since the period of disinterested patriotism is gone by forever. I am certainly far from affirming that in order to obtain this result the exercise of political rights should be immediately granted to all men. But I maintain that the most powerful and perhaps the only means that we still possess of interesting men in the welfare of their country is to make them partakers in the government. At the present time civic zeal seems to me to be inseparable from the exercise of political rights; and I think that the number of citizens will be found to augment or decrease in Europe in proportion as those rights are extended.

How does it happen that in the United States, where the inhabitants have only recently immigrated to the land which they now occupy, and brought neither customs nor traditions with them there; where they met one another for the first time with no previous acquaintance; where, in short, the instinctive love of country can scarcely exist; how does it happen that everyone takes as zealous an interest in the affairs of his township, his county, and the whole state as if they were his own? It is because everyone, in his sphere, takes an active part in the government of society.

The lower orders in the United States understand the influence exercised by the general prosperity upon their own welfare; simple as this observation is, it is too rarely made by the people. Besides, they are accustomed to regard this prosperity as the fruit of their own exertions. The citizen looks upon the fortune of the public as his own, and he labors for the good of the state, not merely from a sense of pride or duty, but from what I venture to term cupidity.

It is unnecessary to study the institutions and the history of the Americans in order to know the truth of this remark, for their manners render it sufficiently evident. As the American participates in all that is done in his country, he thinks himself obliged to defend whatever may be censured in it; for it is not only his country that is then attacked, it is himself. The consequence is that his national pride resorts to a thousand artifices and descends to all the petty tricks of personal vanity. Nothing is more embarrassing in the ordinary intercourse of life than this irritable patriotism of

the Americans. A stranger may be well inclined to praise
many of the institutions of their country, but he begs
permission to blame some things in it, a permission that is
inexorably refused.

America is therefore a free country in which, lest anybody
should be hurt by your remarks, you are not allowed to speak
freely of private individuals or of the state, of the citizens or of
the authorities, of public or of private undertakings, or, in
short, of anything at all except, perhaps, the climate and the
soil; and even then Americans will be found ready to defend
both as if they had cooperated in producing them.

In our times we must choose between the patriotism of all
and the government of a few; for the social force and activity
which the first confers are irreconcilable with the pledges of
tranquility which are given by the second.

The Idea of Rights in the United States

After the general idea of virtue, I know no higher
principle than that of right; or rather these two ideas are
united in one. The idea of right is simply that of virtue
introduced into the political world. It was the idea of right
that enabled men to define anarchy and tyranny, and that
taught them how to be independent without arrogance and to
obey without servility. The man who submits to violence is
debased by his compliance; but when he submits to that right
of authority, which he acknowledges in a fellow creature, he
rises in some measure above the person who gives the
command. There are no great men without virtue; and there
are no great nations—it may almost be added, there would be
no society—without respect for right; for what is a union of
rational intelligent beings who are held together only by the
bond of force?

I am persuaded that the only means which we possess at
the present time of inculcating the idea of right and of
rendering it, as it were, palpable to the senses is to endow all
with the peaceful exercise of certain rights; this is very clearly
seen in children, who are men without the strength and the
experience of manhood. When a child begins to move in the
midst of the objects that surround him, he is instinctively led
to appropriate to himself everything that he can lay his hands

upon; he has no notion of the property of others, but as he gradually learns the value of things and begins to perceive that he may in his turn be despoiled, he becomes more circumspect, and he ends by respecting those rights in others which he wishes to have respected in himself. The principle, which the child derives from the possession of his toys, is taught to the man by the objects which he may call his own. In America, the most democratic of nations, those complaints against property in general, which are so frequent in Europe, are never heard because in America there are no paupers. As everyone has property of his own to defend, everyone recognizes the principle upon which he holds it.

The same thing occurs in the political world. In America, the lowest classes have conceived a very high notion of political rights, because they exercise those rights; and they refrain from attacking the rights of others in order that their own may not be violated. While in Europe the same classes sometimes resist even the supreme power, the American submits without a murmur to the authority of the pettiest magistrate.

This truth appears even in the trivial details of national life. In France few pleasures are exclusively reserved for the higher classes; the poor are generally admitted wherever the rich are received; and they consequently behave with propriety, and respect whatever promotes the enjoyments that they themselves share. In England, where wealth has a monopoly on amusement as well as on power, complaints are made that whenever the poor happen to enter the places reserved for the pleasures of the rich, they do wanton mischief. Can this be wondered at since care has been taken that they should have nothing to lose? The government of a democracy brings the notion of political rights to the level of the humblest citizens, just as the dissemination of wealth brings the notion of property within the reach of all men; to my mind this is one of its greatest advantages. I do not say it is easy to teach men how to exercise political rights, but I maintain that, when it is possible, the effects which result from it are highly important; and I add that, if there ever was a time at which such an attempt ought to be made, that time is now. Do you not see that religious belief is shaken and the divine notion of right is declining, that morality is debased and the notion of moral right is therefore fading away? Argument is substituted for faith, and calculation for the impulses of sentiment. If, in the midst of this disruption, you do not succeed in connecting the notion of right with that of private interest, which is the only immutable point in the human heart, what means will you have of governing the world except by fear? When I am told that the laws are weak and the people are turbulent, that passions are excited and the authority of virtue is paralyzed, and heretofore no measures must be taken to increase the rights of the democracy, I reply that for these very reasons some measures of the kind ought to be taken; and I believe that governments are still more interested in taking them than society at large, for governments may perish, but society cannot die.

But I do not wish to exaggerate the example that America furnishes. There the people were invested with political rights at a time when they could not be abused, for the inhabitants were few in number and simple in their manners. As they have increased the Americans have not augmented the power of the democracy they have rather extended its domain. It cannot be doubted that the moment at which political rights are granted to a people that had before been without them is a very critical one, that the measure, though often necessary, is always dangerous. A child may kill before he is aware of the value of life; and he may deprive another person of his property before he is aware that his own may be taken from him. The lower orders, when they are first invested with political rights, stand in relation to those rights in the same position as the child does to the whole of nature. This truth may be perceived even in America. The states in which the citizens have enjoyed their rights longest are those in which they make the best use of them.

It cannot be repeated too often that nothing is more fertile in prodigies than the art of being free; but there is nothing more arduous than the apprenticeship of liberty. It is not so with despotism. Despotism often promises to make amends for a thousand previous ills; it supports the right, it protects the oppressed, and it maintains public order. The nation is lulled by the temporary prosperity that it produces, until it is roused to a sense of its misery. Liberty, on the contrary, is generally established with difficulty in the midst of storms; it is perfected by civil discord and its benefits cannot be appreciated until it is already old.

Respect for Law in the United States

It is not always feasible to consult the whole people, either directly or indirectly, in the formation of law; but it cannot be denied that, when this is possible, the authority of law is much augmented. This popular origin, which impairs the excellence and the wisdom of legislation, contributes much to increase its power. There is an amazing strength in the expression of the will of a whole people; and when it declares itself, even the imagination of those who would wish to contest it is overawed. The truth of this fact is well known by parties, and they consequently strive to make out a majority whenever they can. If they have not the greater number of voters on their side, they assert that the true majority abstained from voting; and if they are foiled even there, they have recourse to those persons who had no right to vote.

In the United States, except slaves, servants, and paupers supported by the townships, there is no class of persons who do not exercise the elective franchise and who do not indirectly contribute to make the laws. Those who wish to attack the laws must consequently either change the opinion of the nation or trample upon its decision. A second reason, which is still more direct and weighty, may be adduced: in the United States everyone is personally interested in enforcing the obedience of the whole community to the law; for as the minority may shortly rally the majority to its principles, it is interested in professing that respect for the decrees of the legislator which it may soon have occasion to claim for its own. However irksome an enactment may be, the citizen of the United States complies with it, not only because it is the work of the majority but because it is his own, and he regards it as a contract to which he is himself a party.

In the United States, then, that numerous and turbulent multitude does not exist who, regarding the law as their natural enemy, look upon it with fear and distrust. It is impossible, on the contrary, not to perceive that all classes display the utmost reliance upon the legislation of their country and are attached to it by a kind of parental affection.

I am wrong, however, in saying all classes; for as in America the European scale of authority is inverted, there the wealthy are placed in a position analogous to that of the poor in the Old World, and it is the opulent classes who frequently look upon law with suspicion. I have already observed that the advantage of democracy is not, as has been sometimes asserted, that it protects the interests of all, but simply that it protects those of the majority. In the United States, where the poor rule, the rich have always something to fear from the abuse of their power. This natural anxiety of the rich may produce a secret dissatisfaction, but society is not disturbed by it, for the same reason that withholds the confidence of the rich from the legislative authority makes them obey its mandates: their wealth, which prevents them from making the law, prevents them from withstanding it. Among civilized nations, only those who have nothing to lose ever revolt; and if the laws of a democracy are not always worthy of respect, they are always respected; for those who usually infringe the laws cannot fail to obey those which they have themselves made and by which they are benefited; while the citizens who might be interested in their infraction are induced, by their character and station, to submit to the decisions of the legislature, whatever they may be. Besides, the people in America obey the law, not only because it is their own work but also because it may be changed if it is harmful; a law is observed because first, it is a self-imposed evil and secondly, it is an evil of transient duration.

Activity that Pervades All Parts of the Body Politic

On passing from a free country into one which is not free the traveler is struck by the change; in the former all is bustle and activity; in the latter everything seems calm and motionless. In the one, amelioration and progress are the topics of inquiry; in the other, it seems as if the community wished only to repose in the enjoyment of advantages already acquired. Nevertheless, the country which exerts itself so strenuously to become happy is generally more wealthy and prosperous than that which appears so contented with its lot, and when we compare them, we can scarcely conceive how so many new wants are daily felt in the former, while so few seem to exist in the latter.

If this remark is applicable to those free countries, which have preserved monarchical forms and aristocratic institutions, it is still more so to democratic republics. In these states it is not a portion only of the people who endeavor to improve the state of society, but the whole community is engaged in the task; and it is not the exigencies and convenience of a single class for which provision is to be made, but the exigencies and convenience of all classes at once.

It is not impossible to conceive the surprising liberty that the Americans enjoy; some idea may likewise be formed of their extreme equality; but the political activity that pervades the United States must be seen in order to be understood. No sooner do you set foot upon American ground than you are stunned by a kind of tumult; a confused clamor is heard on every side, and a thousand simultaneous voices demand the satisfaction of their social wants. Everything is in motion around you; here the people of one quarter of a town are met to decide upon the building of a church; there the election of a representative is going on; a little farther, the delegates of a district are hastening to the town in order to consult upon some local improvements; in another place, the laborers of a village quit their plows to deliberate upon the project of a road or a public school. Meetings are called for the sole purpose of declaring their disapprobation of the conduct of the government; while in other assemblies citizens salute the authorities of the day as the fathers of their country.

Societies are formed which regard drunkenness as the principal cause of the evils of the state, and solemnly bind themselves to give an example of temperance. The great political agitation of American legislative bodies, which is the only one that attracts the attention of foreigners, is a mere episode, or a sort of continuation, of that universal movement which originates in the lowest classes of the people and extends successively to all the ranks of society. It is impossible to spend more effort in the pursuit of happiness.

It is difficult to say what place is taken up in the life of an inhabitant of the United States by his concern for politics. To take a hand in the regulation of society and to discuss it is his biggest concern and, so to speak, the only pleasure an American knows. This feeling pervades the most trifling habits of life; even the women frequently attend public meetings and listen to political harangues as a recreation from their household labors. Debating clubs are, to a certain extent, a substitute for theatrical entertainments: an American cannot converse, but he can discuss, and his talk falls into a dissertation. He speaks to you as if he was addressing a meeting; and if he should chance to become warm in the discussion, he will say "Gentlemen" to the person with whom he is conversing.

In some countries the inhabitants seem unwilling to avail themselves of the political privileges which the law gives them; it would seem that they set too high a value upon their time to spend it on the interests of the community; and they shut themselves up in a narrow selfishness, marked out by four sunk fences and a quickset hedge. But if an American were condemned to confine his activity to his own affairs, he would be robbed of one half of his existence; he would feel an immense void in the life which he is accustomed to lead, and his wretchedness would be unbearable.

I am persuaded that if ever a despotism should be established in America, it will be more difficult to overcome the habits that freedom has formed than to conquer the love of freedom itself. This ceaseless agitation which democratic government has introduced into the political world influences all social intercourse. I am not sure that, on the whole, this is not the greatest advantage of democracy; and I am less inclined to applaud it for what it does than for what it causes to be done. It is incontestable that the people frequently conduct public business very badly, but it is impossible that the lower orders should take a part in public business without extending the circle of their ideas and quitting the ordinary routine of their thoughts. The humblest individual who cooperates in the government of society acquires a certain degree of self-respect; and as he possesses authority, he can command the services of minds more enlightened than his own. He is canvassed by a multitude of applicants, and in seeking to deceive him in a thousand ways, they really enlighten him. He takes a part in political undertakings, which he did not originate, but which give him a taste for undertakings of the kind. New improvements are daily pointed out to him in the common property, and this gives him the desire of improving that property which is his own. He is perhaps neither happier nor better than those who came before him, but he is better informed and more active. I have no doubt that the democratic institutions of the United States, joined to the physical constitution of the country, are the cause (not the direct, as is so often asserted, but the indirect cause) of the prodigious commercial activity of the inhabitants. It is not created by the laws, but the people learn how to promote it by the experience derived from legislation.

When the opponents of democracy assert that a single man performs what he undertakes better than the government of all, it appears to me that they are right. The government of an individual, supposing an equality of knowledge on either side, is more consistent, more persevering, more uniform, and more accurate in details than that of a multitude, and it selects with more discrimination the men whom it employs. If any deny this, they have never seen a democratic government, or have judged upon partial evidence. It is true that, even when local circumstances and the dispositions of the people allow democratic institutions to exist, they do not display a regular and methodical system of government. Democratic liberty is far from accomplishing all its projects with the skill of an adroit despotism. It frequently abandons them before they have borne their fruits, or risks them when the consequences may be dangerous; but in the end it produces more than any absolute government; if it does fewer things well, it does a greater number of things. Under its sway the grandeur is not in what the public administration does, but in what is done without it or outside of it. Democracy does not give the people the most skillful government, but it produces what the ablest governments are frequently unable to create: namely, an all-pervading and restless activity, a superabundant force, and an energy which is inseparable from it and which may, however unfavorable circumstances may be, produce wonders. These are the true advantages of democracy.

In the present age, when the destinies of Christendom seem to be in suspense, some hasten to assail democracy as a hostile power while it is yet growing; and others already adore this new deity, which is springing forth from chaos. But both parties are imperfectly acquainted with the object of their hatred or their worship; they strike in the dark and distribute their blows at random.

We must first understand what is wanted of society and its government. Do you wish to give a certain elevation to the human mind and teach it to regard the things of this world with generous feelings, to inspire men with a scorn of mere temporal advantages, to form and nourish strong convictions and keep alive the spirit of honorable devotedness? Is it your object to refine the habits, embellish the manners, and cultivate the arts, to promote the love of poetry, beauty, and glory? Would you constitute a people fitted to act powerfully upon all other nations, and prepared for those high enterprises which, whatever be their results, will leave a name forever famous in history? If you believe such to be the principal object of society, avoid the government of the democracy, for it would not lead you with certainty to the goal.

But if you hold it expedient to divert the moral and intellectual activity of man to the production of comfort and the promotion of general well-being; if a clear understanding be more profitable to man than genius; if your object is not to stimulate the virtues of heroism, but the habits of peace; if you had rather witness vices than crimes, and are content to meet with fewer noble deeds, provided offenses be diminished in the same proportion; if, instead of living in the midst of a brilliant society, you are contented to have prosperity around you; if, in short, you are of the opinion that the principal object of a government is not to confer the greatest possible power and glory upon the body of the nation, but to ensure the greatest enjoyment and to avoid the most misery to each of the individuals who compose it—if such be your desire, then equalize the conditions of men and establish democratic institutions.

But if the time is past at which such a choice was possible, and if some power superior to that of man already hurries us, without consulting our wishes, towards one or the other of these two governments, let us endeavor to make the best of that which is allotted to us and, by finding out both its good and its evil tendencies, be able to foster the former and repress the latter to the utmost.

QUESTIONS FOR THOUGHT / DISCUSSION:

> ➤ Toqueville compares and contrasts democracy versus aristocracy in the beginning of this selection. He opines that a sort of tyranny of the minority over the majority is more likely to happen with an aristocracy. Why does he think this is not likely to happen with a democracy?
> ➤ Toqueville claims that people in all social classes in America support their democracy because they all have a stake in the system. How can this be seen to illustrate the symbiotic relationship between capitalism and democracy?
> ➤ Why does Toqueville think that majoritarian democracy is not necessarily a good system?

V. Aristotle:
The Politics

Aristotle (384-322 B.C.) was a Macedonian and student of Plato at the Academy in Athens. He became teacher to Alexander the Great and founded his own school, known as the Lyceum. He was more practical and less idealistic than some, preferring to rely on that which he could see, touch, prove. He was a pragmatist and a realist.

Aristotle contributed much to Western thought and is frequently referred to as the world's first political scientist. However, his range of interests went far beyond the philosophical. He studied, researched, and taught physics, biology, botany, zoology, anatomy, and meteorology. He also had a great interest in psychology, economics, history, poetry, drama, and ethics. Aristotle was well known for his empirical methods of inquiry, basing all of his conclusions on careful study and observation, coupled with reason and logic.

He is also well known for his ethical theories of the Good Life and the Golden Mean. Aristotle believed that man needed to apply his own powers of reasoning to find his own happiness, the good life. And he allowed that most often the good life would be found in the middle ground, the golden mean. Either extreme is a vice and the middle is where the virtue is found. A balanced life and a balanced personality bring the greatest amount of happiness.

Much of Aristotle's works were lost to Europeans during the Dark Ages, but were resurrected again during the Renaissance. Since then, he has been considered possibly the greatest mind the world has ever known.

The Politics was written after examining more than 150 constitutions employed at one time or another by various city-states of ancient Greece. In this we see the value Aristotle placed on empirical research. He studied what was already in existence or had already been tried in order to come up with that system which would best serve the people. He was looking for the good life for society and concluded that: "The good in the sphere of politics is justice, and justice consists in what tends to promote the common interest. General opinion makes this require some sort of equality."

Aristotle's conclusions (which can be found in both his Ethics and Politics) show that he felt a political society based on the rule of law, with a large middle class, practicing a capitalist economic system, and allowing private ownership of property, is what would provide the greatest good for the greatest number.

The following selections were taken from Book IV of The Politics.

Aristotle: The Politics

Chapter I

In all arts and sciences, which embrace the whole of any subject, and do not come into being in a fragmentary way, it is the province of a single art or science to consider all that pertains to a single subject. For example, the art of gymnastics considers not only the suitableness of different modes of training to different bodies, but what sort is absolutely the best—for the absolutely best must suit that which is by nature best and best furnished with the means of life, and also what common form of training is adapted to the great majority of men. And if a man does not desire the best habit of body, or the greatest skill in gymnastics, which might be attained by him, still the trainer or the teacher of gymnastic should be able to impart any lower degree of either. The same principle equally holds in medicine and shipbuilding and the making of clothes and in the arts generally.

Hence it is obvious that government too is the subject of a single science, which has to consider what government is best and of what sort it must be, to be most in accordance with our aspirations, if there were no external impediment, and also what kind of government is adapted to particular states. For the best is often unattainable, and therefore the true legislator and statesman ought to be acquainted, not only with that which is best in the abstract, but also with that which is best relatively to circumstances. We should be able further to say how a state may be constituted under any given conditions; both how it is originally formed and, when formed, how it may be longest preserved, the supposed state being so far from having the best constitution that it is not provided even with the conditions necessary for the best.

He ought, moreover, to know the form of government, which is best suited to states in general; for political writers, although they have excellent ideas, are often unpractical. We should consider, not only what form of government is best, but also what is possible and what is easily attainable by all. There are some who would have none but the most perfect; for this many natural advantages are required. Others, again, speak of a more attainable form, and, although they reject the constitution under which they are living, they extol some one in particular... Any change of government which has to be introduced should be one which men, starting from their existing constitutions, will be both willing and able to adopt, since there is quite as much trouble in the reformation of an old constitution as in the establishment of a new one, just as to unlearn is as hard as to learn. And therefore, in addition to the qualifications of the statesman already mentioned, he should be able to find remedies for the defects of existing constitutions, as has been said before. This he cannot do unless he knows how many forms of government there are.

It is often supposed that there is only one kind of democracy and one of oligarchy. But this is a mistake, and in order to avoid such mistakes, we must ascertain what differences there are in the constitutions of states, and in how many ways they are combined. The same political insight will enable a man to know which laws are the best, and which are suited to different constitutions; for the laws are, and ought to be, relative to the constitution, and not the constitution to the laws. A constitution is the organization of offices in a state, and determines what is to be the governing body, and what is the end of each community. But laws are not to be confounded with the principles of the constitution; they are the rules according to which the magistrates should administer the state and proceed against offenders. So that we must know the varieties, and the number of varieties, of each form of government, if only with a view to making laws. For the same laws cannot be equally suited to all oligarchies or to all democracies, since there is certainly more than one form both of democracy and of oligarchy.

Chapter II

In our original discussion about governments we divided them into three true forms: monarchy, aristocracy, and constitutional government, and three corresponding perversions: tyranny, oligarchy, and democracy. Of monarchy and of aristocracy, we have already spoken, for the inquiry into the perfect state is the same thing with the discussion of the two forms thus named, since both imply a principle of virtue provided with external means. We have already determined in what way aristocracy and monarchy differ from one another, and when the latter should be established. In what follows we have to describe the so-called constitutional government, which bears the common name of all constitutions, and the other forms: tyranny, oligarchy, and democracy.

It is obvious which of the three perversions is the worst, and which is the next worst. That which is the perversion of the first and most divine is necessarily the worst. And just as a monarchy, if not a mere name, must exist by virtue of some great personal superiority in the king, so tyranny, which is the worst of governments, is necessarily the farthest removed from a well-constituted form; oligarchy is little better, for it is a long way from aristocracy, and democracy is the most tolerable of the three.

A writer who preceded me has already made these distinctions, but his point of view is not the same as mine. He lays down the principle that when all the constitutions are good, democracy is the worst, but the best when all are bad. Whereas we maintain that they are in any case defective, and that one oligarchy is not to be accounted better than another, but only less bad.

Not to pursue this question further at present, let us begin by determining how many varieties of constitutions there are, since of democracy and oligarchy there are several. What constitution is the most generally acceptable, and what is eligible in the next degree after the perfect and besides this, what other there is which is aristocratic and well constituted, and at the same time adapted to states in general. Democracy may meet the needs of some better than oligarchy and vice versa. In the next place we have to consider in what manner a man ought to proceed who desires to establish some one among these various forms, whether of democracy or of oligarchy; and lastly, having briefly discussed these subjects to the best of our power, we will endeavor to ascertain the modes of ruin and preservation both of constitutions generally and of each separately, and to what causes they are to be attributed.

Chapter III

The reason why there are so many forms of government is that every state contains many elements. In the first place we see that all states are made up of families, and in the multitude of citizens there must be some rich and some poor, and some in a middle condition; the rich are heavily armed, and the poor not. Of the common people, some are herdsmen, and some traders, and some artisans. There are also differences of wealth and property, for example, in the number of horses which they keep, for they cannot afford to keep them unless they are rich. And therefore in old times the cities whose strength lay in their cavalry were oligarchies, and they used cavalry in wars against their neighbors... Besides differences of wealth there are differences of rank and merit, and there are some other elements, which were mentioned when we discussed aristocracy and enumerated the essentials of a state. Of these elements, sometimes all, sometimes the lesser and sometimes the greater number, have a share in the government.

It is evident then that there must be many forms of government, differing in kind, since the parts of which they are composed differ from each other in kind. For a constitution is an organization of offices, which all the citizens distribute among themselves, according to the power which different classes possess, or according to some principle of equality which includes all. There must therefore be as many forms of government as there are modes of arranging the offices, according to the differences of the parts of the state.

There are generally thought to be two principal forms. As men say of the winds that there are but two—north and south, and that the rest of them are only variations of these—so of governments there are said to be only two forms, democracy and oligarchy. For aristocracy is considered to be a kind of oligarchy, as being the rule of a few, and the constitutional government to be really a democracy, just as among the winds we make the west a variation of the north, and the east of the south wind. Similarly of musical modes there are said to be two kinds, the Dorian and the Phrygian; the other arrangements of the scale are comprehended under one or other of these two. About forms of government this is a very favorite notion. But in either case the better and more exact way is to distinguish, as I have done, the one or two which are true forms, and to regard the others as perversions, whether of the most perfectly tempered mode or of the best form of government: we may compare the more sever and more overpowering modes to be the oligarchic forms, and the more relaxed and gentler ones to be the democratic.

Chapter IV

It must not be assumed, as some are fond of saying, that democracy is simply that form of government in which the greater number are sovereign, for in oligarchies, and indeed in every government, the majority rules; nor again is oligarchy that form of government in which a few are sovereign. Suppose the whole population of a city to be 1300, and that of these, 1000 are rich and do not allow the remaining 300, who are poor but free and in other respects their equals, a share of the government—no one will say that this is a democracy. In like manner, if the poor were few and the masters of the rich who outnumber them, no one would ever call such a government, in which the rich majority have no share of office, an oligarchy. Therefore we should rather say that democracy is the form of government in which the free are rulers, and oligarchy in which the rich are rulers; it is only an accident that the free are the many and the rich are the few. Otherwise a government, in which the offices were given according to stature...or according to beauty, would be an oligarchy; for the number of tall or good-looking men is small. And yet oligarchy and democracy are not sufficiently distinguished merely by these two characteristics of wealth and freedom. Both of them contain many other elements, and therefore we must carry our analysis further, and say that the government is not a democracy in which the freemen, being few in number, rule over the many who are not free... Neither is it a democracy when the rich have the government because they exceed in number... But the form of government is a democracy when the free, who are also poor and the majority, govern, and an oligarchy when the rich and the noble govern, they being at the same time few in number.

I have said that there are many forms of government, and have explained to what causes the variety is due. Why there are more than those already mentioned, and what they are and whence they arise, I will now proceed to consider, starting from the principle already admitted, which is that every state consists, not of one, but of many parts. If we were going to speak of the different species of animals, we should first of all determine the organs which are indispensable to every animal, for example some organs of sense and the instruments of receiving and digesting food, such as the mouth and the stomach, besides organs of locomotion. Assuming now that there are only so many kinds of organs, but that there may be differences in them—I mean different kinds of mouths, and stomachs, and perception and locomotive organs—the possible combinations of these differences will necessarily furnish many varieties of animals, for animals cannot be the same which have different kinds of mouths or of ears. And when all the combinations are exhausted, there will be as many sorts of animals as there are combinations of the necessary organs.

The same then, is true of the forms of government which have been described. States, as I have repeatedly said, are composed not of one, but of many elements. One element is the food-producing class, who are called farmers and herdsmen; a second, the class of mechanics who practice the arts without which a city cannot exist; of these arts some are absolutely necessary, others contribute to luxury. The third class is that of traders, and by traders I mean those who are engaged in buying and selling, whether in commerce or in retail trade. A fourth class is that of the serfs or laborers. The warriors make up the fifth class, and they are as necessary as any of the others, if the country is not to be the slave of every invader...

And as the soul may be said to be more truly part of an animal than the body, so the higher parts of states, that is to say, the warrior class, and the sixth class, which is engaged in the administration of justice and deliberation, the special business of political common sense—these are more essential to the state than the parts which minister to the necessities of life. Whether their several functions are the functions of different citizens or of the same—for it may often happen that the same persons are both warriors and farmers—is immaterial to the argument. The higher as well as the lower elements are to be equally considered parts of the state, and if so, the military element at any rate must be included. There are also the wealthy who minister to the state with their property; these form the seventh class. The eighth class is that of magistrates and of administrators, for the state cannot exist without them. And therefore some must be able to take office and to serve the state, either always or in turn...

If the presence of all these elements and their fair and equitable organization is necessary to states, then there must also be persons who have the ability of statesmen. Different functions appear to be often combined in the same individual; for example, the warrior may also be a farmer or an artisan or a judge. And all claim to possess political ability and think that they are quite competent to fill most offices. But the same persons cannot be rich and poor at the same time. For this reason the rich and the poor are regarded in a special sense as parts of a state. Again, because the rich are generally few in number while the poor are many, they appear to be antagonistic, and as the one or the other prevails they form the government. Hence arises the common opinion that there are two kinds of government—democracy and oligarchy...

Of forms of democracy, first comes that which is said to be based strictly on equality. In such a democracy the law says that it is just for the poor to have no more advantage than the rich, and that neither should be masters, but both equal. For if liberty and equality, as is thought by some, are chiefly to be found in democracy, they will be best attained when all persons alike share in the government to the utmost. And since the people are the majority, and the opinion of the majority is decisive, such a government must necessarily be a democracy. Here then is one sort of democracy. There is another, in which the magistrates are elected according to a certain property qualification, but a low one; he who has the required amount of property has a share in the government, but he who loses his property loses his rights. Another kind is that in which all the citizens who are under no disqualification share in the government, but still the law is supreme. In another, everyone who is a citizen is admitted to the government, but the law is supreme as before. A fifth form of democracy, in other respects the same, is that in which, not the law but the multitude, have the supreme power and supersede the law by their decrees. This is a state of affairs brought about by the demagogues. For in democracies, which are subject to the law, the best citizens hold the first place, and there are no demagogues; but where the laws are not supreme, demagogues spring up. For the people become a monarch, and are many in one, and the many have the power in their hands, not as individuals, but collectively...

At all events this sort of democracy, which is now a monarchy and no longer under the control of law, seeks to exercise absolute power and grows into despotism, this sort of democracy being to other democracies what tyranny is to other forms of monarchy. The spirit of both is the same and they alike exercise a despotic rule over the citizens. The decrees of the demos correspond to the edicts of the tyrant; and the demagogue is to the one what the flatterer is to the other. Both have great power—the flatterer with the tyrant, the demagogue with democracies of the kind which we are describing. The demagogues make the decrees of the people override the laws, by referring all things to the popular assembly. And therefore they grow great, because they hold in their hands the votes of the people, who are too ready to listen to them. Further, those who have any complaint to bring against the magistrates say: "Let the people be judges." The people are too happy to accept the invitation and so the authority of every office is undermined.

Such a democracy is fairly open to the objection that it is not a constitution at all, for where the laws have no authority, there is no constitution. The law ought to be supreme over all, and the magistrates should judge of particulars, and only this should be considered a constitution. So that if democracy be a real form of government, the sort of system in which all things are regulated by decrees is clearly not even a democracy in the true sense of the word, for decrees relate only to particulars.

These then are the different kinds of democracy.

Chapter V

Of oligarchies, too, there are different kinds: one where the property qualification for office is such that the poor, although they form the majority, have no share in the government, yet he who acquires a qualification may obtain a share. Another sort is when there is a qualification for office, but a high one, and the vacancies in the governing body are filled through elections by that body. If the election is made out of all the qualified persons, a constitution of this kind inclines to an aristocracy, if out of a privileged class, to an oligarchy. Another sort of oligarchy is when the son succeeds the father. There is a fourth form, likewise hereditary, in which the magistrates are supreme and not the law...

These are the different sorts of oligarchies and democracies. It should, however, be remembered that in many states the constitution which is established by law, although not democratic, owing to the education and habits of the people may be administered democratically, and conversely in other states the established constitution may incline to democracy, but may be administered in an oligarchic spirit. This most often happens after a revolution, for governments do not change at once. At first the dominant party is content with encroaching a little upon their opponents. The laws, which existed previously, continue in force but the authors of the revolution have the power in their hands.

Chapter VII

There are still two forms besides democracy and oligarchy; one of them is universally recognized and included among the four principal forms of government, which are said to be monarchy, oligarchy, democracy, and the so-called aristocracy or government of the best. But there is also a fifth, which retains the generic name of constitutional government; this is not common, and therefore has not been noticed by writers who attempt to enumerate the different kinds of government...

Chapter VIII

I have yet to speak of the so-called commonwealth and of tyranny. I put them in this order, not because a commonwealth or constitutional government is to be regarded as a perversion any more than the above-mentioned aristocracies. The truth is that they fall short of the most perfect form of government, and so they are reckoned among perversions, and the really perverted forms are perversions of these, as I said in the original discussion. Last of all I will speak of tyranny, which I place last in the series because I am inquiring into the constitutions of states, and this is the very reverse of a constitution.

Having explained why I have adopted this order, I will proceed to consider constitutional government; of which the nature will be clearer now that oligarchy and democracy have been defined. For commonwealth or constitutional government may be described generally as a fusion of oligarchy and democracy; but the term is usually applied to those forms of government which incline towards democracy, and the term aristocracy to those which incline towards oligarchy, because birth and education are commonly the accompaniments of wealth. Moreover, the rich already possess the external advantages the want of which is a temptation to crime, and hence they are called noblemen and gentlemen. And inasmuch as aristcracy seeks to give predominance to the best of the citizens, people say also of oligarchies that they are composed of noblemen and gentlemen.

Now it appears to be an impossible thing that the state, which is governed not by the best citizens but by the worst, should be well governed, and equally impossible that the state, which is ill-governed, should be governed by the best. But we must remember that good laws, if they are not obeyed, do not constitute good government. Hence there are two parts of good government: one is the actual obedience of citizens to the laws, the other part is the goodness of the laws which they obey; they may obey bad laws as well as good...

The distribution of offices according to merit is a special characteristic of aristocracy, for the principle of an aristocracy is virtue, as wealth is of an oligarchy, and freedom of a democracy. In all of them there of course exists the right of the majority, and whatever seems good to the majority of those who share in the government has authority.

Now in a state of this kind there is a constitutional government, for the fusion goes no further than the attempt to unite the freedom of the poor and the wealth of the rich, who commonly take the place of the nobles. But as there are three grounds on which men claim an equal share in the government—freedom, wealth, and virtue—it is clear that the mixture of the two elements, of the free and the wealthy, is to be called a constitutional government; and the union of the three is to be called aristocracy or the government of the best, and more than any other form of government, except the true and ideal, has a right to this name.

Thus far I have shown the existence of forms of states other than monarchy, democracy, and oligarchy, and what they are, and how aristocracies differ from one another, and commonwealths from aristocracies...

Chapter IX

Next we have to consider how by the side of oligarchy and democracy the so-called constitutional government springs up, and how it should be organized. The nature of it will be at once understood from a comparison of oligarchy and democracy; we must ascertain their different characteristics, and taking a portion from each, put the two together like the parts of an indenture. Now there are three modes in which fusions of government may be affected. In the first mode we must combine the laws made by both governments say, concerning the administration of justice. In oligarchies they impose a fine on the rich if they do not serve as judges, and to the poor they give no pay; but in democracies they give pay to the poor and do not fine the rich. Now the union of these two modes is a common or middle term between them, and is therefore characteristic of a constitutional government, for it is a combination of both. This is one mode of uniting the two elements. Or a mean may be taken between the enactments of the two: thus democracies require no property qualification, or only a small one, from members of the assembly, oligarchies a high one; here neither of these is the common term, but a mean between them. There is a third mode, in which something is borrowed from the oligarchic and something from the democratic principle. For example, the appointment of magistrates by lot is thought to be democratic, and the election of them oligarchic; democratic again when there is no property qualification, oligarchic when there is. In the aristocratic or constitutional state, one element will be taken from each—from oligarchy the principle of electing to offices, from democracy the disregard of qualification. Such are the various modes of combination.

There is a true union of oligarchy and democracy when the same state may be termed either a democracy or an oligarchy; those who use both names evidently feel that the fusion is complete. Such a fusion there is also in the mean, for both extremes appear in it. The Lacedaemonian constitution, for example, is often described as a democracy, because it has many democratic features. In the first place the youth receive a democratic education. For the sons of the poor are brought up with the sons of the rich, who are educated in such a manner as to make it possible for the sons of the poor to be educated by them. A similar equality prevails in the following period of life, and when the citizens are grown up to manhood the same rule is observed; there is no distinction between the rich and poor. In like manner they all have the same food at their public tables, and the rich wear only such clothing as any poor man can afford. Again, the people elect to one of the two greatest offices of state, and in the other they share... By others the Spartan constitution is said to be an oligarchy, because it has many oligarchic elements. That all offices are filled by election and none by lot, is one of these oligarchic characteristics; that the power of inflicting death or banishment rests with a few persons is another; and there are others. In a well attempted polity there should appear to be both elements and yet neither; also the government should rely on itself, and not on foreign aid, and on itself not through the good will of a majority—they might be equally well-disposed when there is a vicious form of government—but through the general willingness of all classes in the state to maintain the constitution.

Enough of the manner in which a constitutional government, and in which the so-called aristocracies ought to bo framcd.

Chapter XI

We have now to inquire what is the best constitution for most states, and the best life for most men, neither assuming a standard of virtue which is above ordinary persons, nor an education which is exceptionally favored by nature and circumstances, nor yet an ideal state which is an aspiration only, but having regard to the life in which the majority are able to share, and to the form of government which states in general can attain. As to those aristocracies, as they are called, of which we were just now speaking, they either lie beyond the possibilities of the greater number of states, or they approximate to the so-called constitutional government, and therefore need no separate discussion...

Now in all states there are three elements: one class is very rich, another very poor, and a third in a mean or middle. It is admitted that moderation and the mean are best, and therefore it will clearly be best to possess the gifts of fortune in moderation; for in that condition of life men are most ready to follow rational principle. But he who greatly excels in beauty, strength, birth, or wealth, or on the other hand who is very poor, or very weak, or very much disgraced, finds it difficult to follow rational principle. Of these two the one sort grow into violent and great criminals, the others into rogues and petty rascals. And two sorts of offenses correspond to them, the one committed from violence, the other from roguery.

Again, the middle class is least likely to shrink from rule, or to be over-ambitious for it; both of which are injuries to the state. Again, those who have too much of the goods of fortune, strength, wealth, friends, and the like, are neither willing nor able to submit to authority. The evil begins at home; for when they are boys, by reason of the luxury in which they are brought up, they never learn, even at school, the habit of obedience. On the other hand, the very poor, who are in the opposite extreme, are too degraded. So that the one class cannot obey, and can only rule despotically; the other knows not how to command and must be ruled like slaves.

Thus arises a city, not of freemen, but of masters and slaves, the one despising, the other envying; and nothing can be more fatal to friendship and good fellowship in states than this: for good fellowship springs from friendship; when men are at enmity with one another, they would rather not even share the same path. But a city ought to be composed, as far as possible, of equals, and these are generally the middle classes. Wherefore the city, which is composed of middle class citizens, is necessarily best constituted in respect of the elements of which we say the fabric of the state naturally consists. And this is the class of citizens which is most secure in a state, for they do not, like the poor, covet their neighbors' goods; nor do others covet theirs, as the poor covet the goods of the rich; and as they neither plot against others, nor are themselves plotted against, they pass through life safely...

Thus it is manifest that the best political community is formed by citizens of the middle class, and that those states are likely to be well-administered in which the middle class is large, and stronger if possible than both the other classes, or at any rate than either singly; for the addition of the middle class turns the scale, and prevents either of the extremes from being dominant.

Great then is the good fortune of a state in which the citizens have a moderate and sufficient property; for where some possess much, and the others nothing, there may arise an extreme democracy, or a pure oligarchy; or a tyranny may grow out of either extreme—either out of the most rampant democracy, or out of an oligarchy; but it is not so likely to arise out of the middle constitutions and those akin to them...The mean condition of states is clearly best, for no other is free from faction; and where the middle class is large, there are least likely to be factions and dissensions. For a similar reason large states are less liable to faction than small ones, because in them the middle class is large; whereas in small states it is easy to divide all the citizens into two classes who are either rich or poor, and to leave nothing in the middle.

And democracies are safer and more permanent than oligarchies, because they have a middle class, which is more numerous and has a greater share in the government; for when there is no middle class, and the poor greatly exceed in number, troubles arise, and the state soon comes to an end. A proof of the superiority of the middle class is that the best legislators have been of a middle condition...

These considerations will help us to understand why most governments are either democratic or oligarchic. The reason is that the middle class is seldom numerous in them, and whichever party, whether the rich or the common people, transgresses the mean and predominates, draws the constitution its own way, and thus arises either oligarchy or democracy. There is another reason—the poor and the rich quarrel with one another, and whichever side gets the better, instead of establishing a just or popular government, regards political supremacy as the prize of victory, and the one party sets up a democracy and the other an oligarchy. Further, both the parties which had the supremacy in Hellas looked only to the interest of their own form of government, and established in states, the one, democracies, and the other, oligarchies; they thought of their own advantage, of the public not at all. For these reasons the middle form of government has rarely, if ever, existed, and among a very few only. One man alone of all who ever ruled in Hellas was induced to give this middle constitution to states. But it has now become a habit among the citizens of states, not even to care about equality; all men are seeking for dominion, or, if conquered, are willing to submit.

What then is the best form of government, and what makes it the best, is evident; and of other constitutions, since we say that there are many kinds of democracy and many of oligarchy, it is not difficult to see which has the first and which the second or any other place in the order of excellence, now that we have determined which is the best. For that which is nearest to the best must of necessity be better, and that which is furthest from it worse, if we are judging absolutely and not relatively to given conditions: I say 'relatively to given conditions,' since a particular government may be preferable, but another form may be better for some people.

Chapter XIV

Having thus gained an appropriate basis of discussion, we will proceed to speak of the points which follow next in order. We will consider the subject not only in general but with reference to particular constitutions. All constitutions have three elements, concerning which the good lawgiver has to regard what is expedient for each constitution. When they are well-ordered, the constitution is well-ordered, and as they differ from one another, constitutions differ. There is one element which deliberates about public affairs; second, that concerned with the magistrates—the question being what they should be, over what they should exercise authority, and what should be the mode of electing them; and third, that which has judicial power.

The deliberative element has authority in matters of war and peace, in making and unmaking alliances; it passes laws, inflicts death, exile, confiscation, elects magistrates and audits their accounts. These powers must be assigned either all to all the citizens, or all to some, or some of them to all, and others of them only to some. That all things should be decided by all is characteristic of democracy; this is the sort of equality which the people desire. But there are various ways in which all may share in the government; they may deliberate, not all in one body, but by turns...

There are other constitutions in which the boards of magistrates meet and deliberate, but come into office by turns, and are elected out of the tribes and the very smallest divisions of the state, until every one has obtained office in his turn. The citizens, on the other hand, are assembled only for the purposes of legislation, and to consult about the constitution, and to hear the edicts of the magistrates. In another variety of democracy the citizens form one assembly, but meet only to elect magistrates, to pass laws, to advise about war and peace... Other matters are referred severally to special magistrates, who are elected by vote or by lot out of all the citizens. Or again, the citizens meet about election to offices and deliberate concerning war or alliances while other matters are administered by the magistrates, who, as far as is possible, are elected by vote. I am speaking of those magistracies in which special knowledge is required.

A fourth form of democracy is when all the citizens meet to deliberate about everything, and the magistrates decide nothing, but only make the preliminary inquiries; and that is the way in which the last and worst form of democracy, corresponding, as we maintain, to the close family oligarchy and to tyranny, is at present administered. All these modes are democratic.

On the other hand, that some should deliberate about all is oligarchic. This again is a mode which, like the democratic, has many forms. When the deliberative class, being elected out of those who have a moderate qualification, are numerous and they respect and obey the prohibitions of the law without altering it, and any one who has the required qualification shares in the government, then just because of this moderation, the oligarchy inclines towards polity. But when only selected individuals and not the whole people share in the deliberations of the state, then, although as in the former case they observe the law, the government is a pure oligarchy. Or, again, when those who have the power of deliberation are self-elected, and son succeeds father, and they and not the laws are supreme—the government is of necessity oligarchic. Where, again, particular persons have authority in particular matters—for example, when the whole people decide about peace and war, but the magistrates regulate everything else, and they are elected by vote—there the government is an aristocracy. And if some questions are decided by magistrates elected by vote, and others by magistrates elected by lot, either absolutely or out of select candidates, or elected partly by vote, partly by lot, these practices are partly characteristic of an aristocratic government, and part of a pure constitutional government.

These are the various forms of the deliberative body; they correspond to the various forms of government. And the government of each state is administered according to one or other of the principles which have been laid down. Now it is for the interest of democracy, according to the most prevalent notion of it. I am speaking of that extreme form of democracy in which the people are supreme even over the laws, with a view to better deliberation to adopt the custom of oligarchies respecting courts of law. For in oligarchies the rich who are wanted to be judges are compelled to attend under pain of a fine, whereas in democracies the poor are paid to attend. And this practice of oligarchies should be adopted by democracies in their public assemblies, for they will advise better if they all deliberate together—the people with the notables and the notables with the people.

It is also a good plan that those who deliberate should be elected by vote or by lot in equal numbers out of the different classes; and that if the people greatly exceed in number those who have political training, pay should not be given to all, but only to as many as would balance the number of the notables, or that the number in excess should be eliminated by lot...Again, in oligarchies either the people ought to accept the measures of the government, or not to pass anything contrary to them; or, if all are allowed to share in counsel, the decision should rest with the magistrates. The opposite of what is done in constitutional governments should be the rule in oligarchies; the veto of the majority should be final, their assent not final, but the proposal should be referred back to the magistrates. Whereas in constitutional governments they take the contrary course; the few have the negative, not the affirmative power; the affirmation of everything rests with the multitude.

These, then, are our conclusions respecting the deliberative, that is, the supreme element in states.

Chapter XV

Next we will proceed to consider the distribution of offices; this too, being a part of politics concerning which many questions arise: What shall their number be? Over what shall they preside, and what shall be their duration? Sometimes they last for six months, sometimes for less; sometimes they are annual, while in other cases offices are held for still longer periods. Shall they be for life or for a long term of years; or, if for a short term only, shall the same persons hold them over and over again, or once only? Also about the appointment to them—from whom are they to be chosen, by whom, and how?

We should first be in a position to say what are the possible varieties of them, and then we may proceed to determine which are suited to different forms of government. But what are to be included under the term 'offices?' That is a question not quite so easily answered. For a political community requires many officers, and not every one who is chosen by vote or by lot is to be regarded as a ruler. In the first place there are the priests, who must be distinguished from political officers; masters of choruses and heralds, even ambassadors, are elected by vote. Some duties of superintendence again are political, extending either to all the citizens in a single sphere of action, like the office of the general who superintends them when they are in the field, or to a section of them only, like the inspectorships of women or of youth. Other offices are concerned with household management, like that of the corn measurers who exist in many states and are elected officers. There are also menial offices which the rich have executed by their slaves. Speaking generally, those are to be called offices to which the duties are assigned of deliberating about certain measures and of judging and commanding, especially the last, for to command is the especial duty of a magistrate. But the question is not of any importance in practice; no one has ever brought into court the meaning of the word, although such problems have a speculative interest.

What kinds of offices, and how many, are necessary to the existence of a state, and which, if not necessary, yet conduce to its well-being are much more important considerations, affecting all constitutions, but more especially small states. For in great states it is possible, and indeed necessary, that every office should have a special function; where the citizens are numerous, many may hold office. And so it happens that some offices a man holds a second time only after a long interval, and others he holds once only; and certainly every work is better done which receives the sole, and not the divided attention of the worker.

But in small states it is necessary to combine many offices in a few hands, since the small number of citizens does not admit of many holding office: for who will there be to succeed them? And yet small states at times require the same offices and laws as large ones; the difference is that the one want them often, the others only after long intervals. Hence there is no reason why the care of many offices should not be imposed on the same person, for they will not interfere with each other...

We must first ascertain how many magistrates are necessary in every state, and also how many are not exactly necessary, but are nevertheless useful, and then there will be no difficulty in seeing what offices can be combined in one. We should also know over which matters several local tribunals are to have jurisdiction, and in which authority should be centralized: for example, should one person keep order in the market and another in some other place, or should the same person be responsible everywhere? Again, should offices be divided according to the subjects with which they deal, or according to the persons with whom they deal...?

Further, under different constitutions, should the magistrates be the same or different? For example, in democracy, oligarchy, aristocracy, monarchy, should there be the same magistrates, although they are elected, not out of equal or similar classes of citizen but differently under different constitutions: in aristocracies, for example, they are chosen from the educated, in oligarchies from the wealthy, and in democracies from the free—or are there certain differences in the offices answering to them as well, and may the same be suitable to some, but different offices to others? For in some states it may be convenient that the same office should have a more extensive, in other states a narrower sphere...

Even the power of the council disappears when democracy has taken that extreme form in which the people themselves are always meeting and deliberating about everything. This is the case when the members of the assembly receive abundant pay, for they have nothing to do and are always holding assemblies and deciding everything for themselves...

Chapter XVI

Of the three parts of government, the judicial remains to be considered, and this we shall divide on the same principle. There are three points on which the varieties of law-courts depend: The persons from whom they are appointed, the matters with which they are concerned, and the manner of their appointment. I mean: are the judges taken from all, or from some only? How many kinds of law-courts are there? Are the judges chosen by vote or by lot?

First, let me determine how many kinds of law-courts there are. There are eight in number: One is the court of audits; a second takes cognizance of ordinary offenses against the state; a third is concerned with treason against the constitution; the fourth determines disputes respecting penalties, whether raised by magistrates or by private persons; the fifth decides the more important civil cases; the sixth tries cases of homicide, which are of various kinds: premeditated, involuntary, cases in which the guilt is confessed but the justice is disputed; and there may be a fourth court in which murderers who have fled from justice are tried after their return... But cases of this sort rarely happen at all even in large cities. The different kinds of homicide may be tried either by the same or by different courts. There are courts for strangers: of these there are two subdivisions: for the settlement of their disputes with one another, and for the settlement of disputes between them and the citizens. And besides all these there must be courts for small suits about sums of a drachma up to five drachmas, or a little more, which have to be determined, but they do not require many judges.

Nothing more need be said of these small suits, nor of the courts for homicide and for strangers: I would rather speak of political cases, which, when mismanaged, create division and disturbances in constitutions...

In how many forms law-courts can be established has now been considered. The first form, that in which the judges are taken from all the citizens, and in which all causes are tried, is democratic; the second, which is composed of a few only who try all causes, oligarchic; the third, in which some courts are taken from all classes, and some from certain classes only, aristocratic and constitutional.

QUESTIONS FOR THOUGHT / DISCUSSION:

➢ Aristotle seems to believe that a constitutional form of government is the best and the middle class is the best group to rule. What is it about the middle class that he thinks is so much better than the lower or upper classes?

➢ Do you recognize our system of three branches of government with a separation of powers in this selection? What are the branches Aristotle's discusses and the functions of each?

➢ What would Madison have to say about Aristotle's opinion of and remedy for factions?

VI. Thomas Aquinas:
The Governance of Rulers

Thomas Aquinas (1225-1274) was a Dominican monk in the Middle Ages who divided his time between Rome, Naples, and Paris. He was a philosopher, teacher, author, and devotee of Aristotle. He undertook to explain many of Aristotle's works in the form of commentaries. These works had only recently resurfaced in medieval Europe and many were being challenged as incompatible with Christian beliefs.

One of the most significant among all of Aquinas' accomplishments was his effort to reconcile the antagonism between faith and reason. Science was advancing during his lifetime and religious faith was being challenged by these advances. Aquinas reasoned that a search for truth through reason was in fact a search for God, since he was the source of all truth. Aquinas said that while man was capable of learning much through his observations, his sense, his logic, all of the things he observed were created by God and so there really was no conflict between faith and reason. He also allowed that even though man was capable of understanding many of the divine mysteries through the use of reason and natural intellect, there were still many things beyond man's intellectual capacity and those things must simply be taken on faith.

Aquinas became known as the official philosopher of the Catholic Church and his Summa Theologica, a textbook he wrote for theology students, is recognized as his greatest work, and still widely read today by theology students. The Catholic Church declared him a saint in 1323.

The selection reprinted here is from one of the few treatises Aquinas ever wrote on political matters. Much of his study of Aristotle can be seen in this work. Aquinas believed that by living in a political society men would benefit from the knowledge shared with others. Since no one person could possibly know everything, each member of society would contribute some part of the total knowledge of the group and they would all gain; the whole is greater than the sum of its parts. Indeed, the only reason for a society to come together is for the purpose of achieving common goals.

Thomas Aquinas: The Governance Of Rulers

Men in Society Must be Under Rulers

We must first explain what is meant by the term, king. When a thing is directed towards an end, and it is possible to go one way or another, someone must indicate the best way to proceed toward the end. For example, a ship that moves in different directions with the shifting winds would never reach its destination if it were not guided into port by the skill of its helmsman. Man, too, has an end toward which all the actions of his life are directed, since all intelligent beings act for an end. Yet the diversity of men's pursuits and activities means that men proceed to their intended objectives in different ways. Therefore man needs someone to direct him towards his end. Now every man is naturally endowed with the light of reason to direct his actions towards his end. If men were intended to live alone as do many animals, there would be no need for anyone to direct him towards his end, since every man would be his own king under God, the highest king, and the light of reason given to him from on high would enable him to act on his own. But man is by nature a political and social animal. Even more than other animals he lives in groups. This is demonstrated by the requirements of his nature. Nature has given other animals food, furry covering, teeth, and horns and claws—or at least speed of flight—as means to defend themselves. Man however, is given none of these by nature. Instead he has been given the use of his reason to secure all these things by the work of his hands. But a man cannot secure all these by himself, for a man cannot adequately provide for his life by himself. Therefore it is natural for man to live in association with his fellows.

In addition, nature has installed in other animals the ability to perceive what is useful or harmful to them. For example, a sheep knows by nature that the wolf is its enemy. Some animals even have the natural ability to know the medicinal herbs and other things necessary to their existence.

Man, on the other hand, has a natural knowledge of what is necessary to his life only in a general way, using his reason to move from general principles to the knowledge of particular things that are necessary for human life. And it is not possible for one man to arrive at the knowledge of all these things through the use of his reason. Thus it is necessary for him to live in society so that one person can help another and different men can employ their reasons in different ways, one in medicine, and others in this or that endeavor. This is most clearly demonstrated by the fact that man uses words to communicate his thoughts fully to others. It is true that other animals express their feelings in a general way. Dogs express their anger by barking and other animals express their feelings in other ways. But man is more able to communicate with others than other gregarious animals such as cranes, ants, or bees. Solomon refers to this when he says, "It is better for two to live together than alone, for they have the advantage of mutual company."

Therefore, since it is natural for man to live in association with others there must be some way for them to be governed. For if many men were to live together and each to provide what is convenient for himself, the group would break up unless one of them had the responsibility for the good of the group, just as the body of a man or an animal would disintegrate without a single controlling force in the body that aimed at the common good of all the members. As Solomon says, "Where there is no ruler, the people will be dispersed." This is reasonable since the private good and the common good are not the same. Private concerns divide the community, while common concerns unite it. Those differences exist for different reasons. Therefore, besides what moves each person to his own private good there must be something that moves everyone to the common good of the many. Therefore in everything that is ordered to a single end, one thing is found that rules the rest. In the physical universe, by the intention of divine providence all the other bodies are ruled by the first or heavenly body, as divine providence directs, and all material bodies are ruled by rational creatures. In each man the soul rules the body and within the soul reason rules over passion and desire. Likewise among the parts of the body there is one ruling part, either the heart or the head that moves all the others. So in every group, there must be something that rules.

When things are ordered to some end, one can proceed in the right way and the wrong way. So the government of a group can be carried out in the right way or the wrong way. Something is done in the right way when it is led to its appropriate end, and in the wrong way when it is led to an inappropriate end. The proper end of a group of free men is different from that of a group of slaves, for a free man determines his own actions while a slave is one who belongs to another. If then a group of free men is directed by a ruler to the common good of the group, his government will be right and just because it is appropriate for free men, but if the government is directed not at the common good of the group but at the private good of the ruler it will be unjust and a perversion. God warns such rulers in the Book of Ezekiel, "Woe to shepherds that feed themselves, because they seek their own benefit. Should not the flocks be fed by the shepherd?" Shepherds must seek the good of their flocks, and rulers, the good of those subject to them.

If a government is under one man who seeks his own benefit and not the good of those subject to him, the ruler is called a tyrant. The word is derived from the Greek word for "strength," because he uses force to oppress the people instead of justice to rule. Hence among the ancients all-powerful men were called tyrants. But if an unjust government is exercised not by one but by more than one, if they are few it is called an oligarchy, which means, "rule by the few." In this case a few rich men oppress the people. Such a government differs only in number from a tyranny. An unjust government exercised by the many is called a democracy, that is, "rule by the people," which occurs when the common people use the force of numbers to oppress the rich. In this case the whole people acts like a tyrant.

We can also classify the types of just government. If the government is carried out by a large number, as when a group of warriors governs a city or province, it is usually called a polity. But if a few virtuous men carry out the administration, a government of this kind is called an aristocracy, that is the best rule, or rule of the best, who for this reason are called the aristocrats. But if a good government is in the hands of one man alone, it is appropriate to call him a king. ...Thus it is very clear that it is the nature of kingship that there should be one to rule and that he should be a shepherd who seeks the common good of all and not his own benefit.

Since men must live together because they cannot acquire what is needed to live if they remain by themselves, a social group is more perfect if it provides better for the necessities of life. A family in a single household provides adequately for some of the needs of life such as the natural acts of nourishment and the procreation of children, etc. In a single locality you will find self-sufficiency in a given manufacture. But a city which is a perfect community contains whatever is needed for life... Therefore the right name for someone who rules a perfect community, whether a city or a province, is a king, while someone who directs a household is not called a king but the father of a family. Yet there is a certain resemblance to a king in his position so that sometimes kings are called the fathers of their people...

Is it Better to be Under One Ruler or Many

Next we must inquire as to whether it is better for a province or a city to be ruled by one person or by many. We will approach this question from the point of view of the purpose of government.

The aim of any ruler should be to promote the welfare of the territory that he has been given to rule. ...The welfare of any organized group is based on the preservation of its unity in what we call peace. Without peace life in society is no longer beneficial and its divisions make social life burdensome. Thus the most important responsibility of the ruler of a community is to achieve unity in peace, just as a doctor does not debate whether to cure a sick man under his care there is no reason for a ruler to question whether he should maintain the peace of the community under him. No one should debate about the end of an action but about the appropriate means. ...Thus the more effective a government is in promoting unity in peace, the more useful it will be. We say more useful, because it leads more directly to its end. But it is evident that that which is only one, can promote unity better than that which is a plurality, just as the most effective cause of heat is that which is in itself hot. Therefore, government by one person is better than by many.

Furthermore, it is evident that many persons cannot preserve the unity of a group if they generally disagree. Some agreement among them is necessary for them to govern at all. A number of men could not move a ship in one direction unless they worked together in some way. But a number of people are said to be united to the extent that they come closer to unity. It is better therefore for one person to rule than for many to try to achieve unity.

In addition, whatever is in accord with nature is best, for nature always operates for the best. But in nature government is always by one. Among the members of the body, the heart moves all the other parts; among the parts of the soul one power, reason, predominates. Among the bees there is one king bee, and in the whole universe one God is the Maker and Ruler of all. This is in accord with reason since every plurality derives from unity. Therefore since art imitates nature and a work of art is better to the degree that it resembles what is in nature, it follows that it is best for a human group to be ruled by one person.

This is also apparent from experience. Provinces and cities that are not ruled by one person are torn by dissension and disputes without peace...

Rule by One Person is the Best Government

Just as government by a king is best, so government by a tyrant is the worst. Democracy stands in opposition to polity as indicated above, since both are governments by the many. Oligarchy is opposed to aristocracy, since both are governments by the few. Kingship is the opposite of tyranny since both are governments by one person. We have shown above that kingship is the best form of government. Since that which is opposite to the best is the worst, it follows that tyranny is worst form of government.

In addition a force that is united is more effective than one that is divided. Many persons working together can pull a load that individually they could not pull. Thus just as a force operating for good is better at producing good if it is one, so a force operating for evil is more harmful if it is one rather than divided. The power of an unjust ruler operates to the detriment of the group because he replaces the common good of the group with his own advantage. Similarly in good governments, since a more unified government is a more effective one, monarchy is better than aristocracy, and aristocracy is better than polity, while in bad governments the opposite is the case so that the more unified it is the more harmful it is. Thus tyranny is more harmful than oligarchy and oligarchy is more harmful than democracy.

Furthermore what makes a government unjust is the fact that the private interest of the ruler is pursued in preference to the common good of the society. The further he departs from the common good, the more unjust his government will be. An oligarchy departs from the common good more than a democracy because it seeks the good of the few rather than the many. Tyranny departs still more from the common good because it seeks the good of only one person. The greater number comes nearer to the whole than a few, and the few nearer than only one person. Tyranny therefore is the most unjust form of government.

We can see this when we consider the order of divine providence, which directs everything in the best way. The good in things results from a single perfect cause, that is, from everything working together for good, while evil results from individual defects. There is no beauty in a body unless all its parts are properly integrated. Ugliness results from one member not fitting in properly. And so ugliness comes in different ways from many different causes while beauty comes in one way from a single perfect cause. In all cases of good and evil God seems to provide that good from one cause will be stronger and evil from many causes will be weaker. It is proper therefore, that a just government should be exercised by one person so that it can be stronger. But if the government becomes unjust it is better that it be exercised by many, so that it is weaker because of internal divisions. Therefore among unjust governments democratic government is the most tolerable of the unjust forms of government, while tyranny is the worst.

This is also apparent when one considers the evils that result from tyranny. The tyrant despises the common good and seeks his private good and as a result he oppresses his subjects in different ways and which goods will be affected will depend on the various passions to which he is subject. If he is subject to the passion of greed, he steals the property of his subjects. ...If he is dominated by the passion of anger, he sheds blood for nothing... The wise man advises us to avoid this kind of government when he says "keep away from the man with the power to kill," for he does not kill in pursuit of justice but uses his power to satisfy his willful lust.

Thus when the ruler departs from law there is no security and everything is uncertain. No reliance can be placed on the will, not to speak of the lust, of another. He threatens not only the bodies of his subjects but also their spiritual welfare, since those who seek to use rather than to be of use to their subjects oppose any progress by their subjects since they suspect that any excellence among their subjects is a threat to their unjust rule. Tyrants always suspect the good rather than the evil and are always afraid of virtue. They seek to prevent their subjects from becoming virtuous and developing a public spiritedness which would not tolerate their unjust domination. They prevent the bond of friendship from developing among their subjects...since as long as there is mutual distrust no attempt can be made to overthrow their rule. Therefore tyrants sow discord among them, promote dissension, and prohibit gatherings such as marriage celebrations and feasts and the like that foster familiarity and mutual trust among men. They try to prevent their subjects from becoming powerful or rich since, judging their subjects on the basis of their own bad consciences, they suspect that they will also use their power and wealth to harm them...

Thus it is that because rulers, instead of inducing their subjects to be virtuous, are wickedly jealous of their virtue and hinder it as much as they can, very few virtuous men are found under tyrants. For as Aristotle says, "Brave men are found where brave men are honored," and Cicero says, "What is despised by everyone decays and ceases to grow." It is natural that men who are brought up in fear should become servile in spirit and cowardly in the face of any difficult or strenuous endeavor. ...So men hide from tyrants as from cruel beasts and there is no difference between being subject to a tyrant and being ravaged by a wild beast.

QUESTIONS FOR THOUGHT / DISCUSSION:

- ➤ Do you agree with Aquinas that a single king as ruler is best? He claims a king is better than a tyrant. Can a king be a tyrant?
- ➤ When he speaks of democracy as a bad system of government, Aquinas is not speaking about the type of democracy we think of when we hear that word. He is speaking of a tyranny of the majority over the minority. James Madison would agree with him that a democracy is not a good system. What does Madison have to say about this topic?
- ➤ What does Aquinas think is the absolute reason for having a government in the first place?

VII. Marcus Cicero: On The Laws

Marcus Cicero (106-43 B.C.) was a Stoic, statesman, and one of the great orators of the Roman Empire, as well as a contemporary of Julius Caesar and Pompey. Stoics believed in an ethical life marked by self-discipline and moderation in all things. The belief in natural rights, reason, and equality are part of the basic philosophy behind Stoicism. The Stoic philosophy had a tremendous influence on the development of Roman Law, allowing that the law is not something created by man as much as it is simply based on reason and logic and the natural laws of the universe. The law, therefore, is the same no matter who you are or where you are.

Cicero's writings reflect his belief that man is a reasonable being, capable of learning, and knowledge is closely connected with virtue. He was not a believer in a majoritarian form of democracy, however, because he feared that the people, as a whole, might act rashly. He believed that the wisest men in a society had a civic duty to rule for the good of all. He was not a believer in dictatorship, though, as Julius Caesar and Marc Antony could attest. He was a proponent of republicanism, representative democracy.

This treatise from Cicero was originally written in the form of a dialogue between Cicero and Quintus. It has been edited here and the comments of Quintus have been eliminated. The excerpts reprinted here outline the philosophy of Cicero on the concept of law and were taken from Books II and III.

Marcus Cicero: On The Laws

Therefore, as that reason is the supreme law, so it exists in the mind of the sage, so far as it can be perfected in man. But with respect to civil laws, which are drawn up in various forms and framed to meet the occasional requirements of the people, the name of law belongs to them not so much by right

as by the favor of the people. For men prove by some such
arguments as the following, that every law which deserves
the name of a law, ought to be morally good and laudable. It
is clear that laws were originally made for the security of the
people, for the preservation of states, for the peace and
happiness of society; and that they who first framed
enactments of that kind persuaded the people that they would
write and publish such laws only as should conduce to the
general morality and happiness, if they would receive and
obey them. And then such regulations, being thus settled and
sanctioned, they justly entitled Laws. From which we may
reasonably conclude, that those who made unjustifiable and
pernicious enactments for the people, acted in a manner
contrary to their own promises and professions, and
established anything rather than laws, properly so called,
since it is evident that the very signification of the word "law"
comprehends the whole essence and energy of justice and
equity. I would, therefore, interrogate you on this point.... If a
state wants something for the want of which it is reckoned no
state at all, must not that something be something good?
...And if a state has no law, is it not for that reason to be
reckoned no state at all? ...We must therefore reckon law
among the very best things...

If, then, in the majority of nations, many pernicious and
mischievous enactments are made, which have no more right
to the name of law than the mutual engagement of robbers,
are we bound to call them laws? For as we cannot call the
recipes of ignorant and unskillful empirics, who give poisons
instead of medicines, the prescriptions of a physician, so
likewise we cannot call that the true law of a people, of
whatever kind it may be, if it enjoins what is injurious, let the
people receive it as they will. For law is the just distinction
between right and wrong, made conformable to that most
ancient nature of all, the original and principal regulator of
all things, by which the laws of men should be measured,
whether they punish the guilty or protect and preserve the
innocent...

For when once our minds are confirmed in these views, it
will not be difficult to inspire them with true and useful
sentiments. For what can be more true than that no man
should be so madly presumptuous as to believe that he has

either reason or intelligence, while he does not believe that the heaven and the world possess them likewise, or to think that those things which he can scarcely comprehend by the greatest possible exertion of his intellect, are put in motion without the agency of reason?

In truth, we can scarcely reckon him a man, whom neither the regular courses of the stars, nor the alterations of day and night, nor the temperature of the seasons, nor the productions that nature displays for his use and enjoyment, urge to gratitude towards heaven.

And as those beings which are furnished with reason are incomparably superior to those which want it, and as we cannot say, without impiety, that anything is superior to the universal nature, we must therefore confess that divine reason is contained within her. And who will dispute the utility of these sentiments, when he reflects how many cases of the greatest importance are decided by oaths; how much the sacred rites performed in making treaties tend to assure peace and tranquility; and what numbers of people the fear of divine punishment has reclaimed from a vicious course of life; and how sacred the social rights must be in a society where a firm persuasion obtains the immediate intervention of the immortal gods, both as witnesses and judges of our actions? Such is the "preamble of the law," to use the expression of Plato...

You see, then, that this is the duty of magistrates, to superintend and prescribe all things, which are just and useful and in accordance with the law. For as the law is set over the magistrate, even so are the magistrates set over the people. And, therefore, it may be truly said that the magistrate is a speaking law, and the law is a silent magistrate. Moreover, nothing is so conformable to justice and to the condition of nature—and when I use that expression, I wish it to be understood that I mean the law and nothing else—as sovereign power without which, neither house nor commonwealth nor nation, nor mankind itself, nor the entire nature of things, nor the universe itself, could exist. For this universe is obedient to God and land and sea are submissive to the universe; and human life depends on the just administration of the laws of the universe; and human life depends on the just administration of the laws of order.

But to come to considerations nearer home, and more familiar to us, all ancient nations have been at one time or other under the dominion of kings, which kind of authority was at first conferred on the wisest of men. Afterward, the authority of kings was handed down in succession to their descendants, and this practice remains to this day in those nations which are governed by kings. And even those to whom the regal domination was distasteful, did not desire to be obedient to no one, but only to be always under the authority of the same person.

For ourselves, then, as we are proposing laws for a free people...we shall on the present occasion endeavor to accommodate our laws to that constitutional government of which we have expressed our approval.

It is clear, then, that magistrates are absolutely necessary, since, without their prudence and diligence, a state cannot exist; and since it is by their regulations that the whole commonwealth is kept within the bounds of moderation. But it is not enough to prescribe them a rule of domination, unless we likewise prescribe the citizens a rule of obedience. For he who commands well, must at some time or other have obeyed; and he who obeys with modesty appears worthy of some day or other being allowed to command. It is desirable, therefore, that he who obeys should expect that some day he will come to command, and that he who commands should bear in mind that before long he may be called to submission...

Let all authorities be just and let them be honestly obeyed by the people with modesty and without opposition. Let the magistrate restrain the disobedient and mischievous citizen by fine, imprisonment, and corporal chastisement, unless some equal or greater power, or the people forbid it—for there should be an appeal thereto. If the magistrate shall have decided and inflicted a penalty, let there be a public appeal to the people respecting the penalty and fine imposed.

With respect to the army and the general who commands it by martial law, there should be no appeal from his authority. And whatever he who conducts the war commands shall be absolute law and ratified as such. As to the minor magistrates, let there be such a distribution of their legal duties that each may more effectively superintend his own department of justice. In the army let those who are appointed command and let them have tribunes. In the city let men be appointed as superintendents of the public treasury. Let some devote their attention to the prison discipline and capital punishments. Let others supervise the public coinage of gold, and silver, and copper. Let others judge suits and arbitrations and carry the orders of the senate into execution. Let there likewise be curators of the city, the provisions, and the public games, and let these offices be the first steps to higher promotions of honor.

Let the censors take a census of the people, according to age, offspring, family, and property. Let them have the inspection of the temples, the streets, the aqueducts, the rates, and the customs. Let them distribute the citizens, according to their tribes; after that let them divide them with reference to their fortunes, ages, and ranks. Let them keep a register of the families of those of the equestrian and plebeian orders. Let them impose a tax on celibates. Let them guard the morals of the people. Let them permit no scandal in the senate. Let the number of such censors be two. Let their magistracy continue five years. Let the other magistrates be annual, but their offices themselves should be perpetual.

Let the judge of the law who shall decide private actions— or send them for decision to the praetor—be the proper guardian of civil jurisprudence. Let him have as many colleagues of equal power as the senate thinks necessary and the people allow.

Let two magistrates be invested with sovereign authority for their presiding, judging, and counseling; let them be called praetors, judges, or consuls. Let them have supreme authority over the army and let them be subject to none, for the safety of the people is the supreme law and no one should succeed to this magistracy till it has been held ten years—regulating the duration by an annual law.

When a considerable war is undertaken or discord is likely to ensue among the citizens, let a single supreme magistrate be appointed, who shall unite in his own person the authority of both consuls, if the senate so decrees, for six months only. And when such a magistrate has been proclaimed under favorable auspices, let him be the master of the people. Let him have for a colleague, with equal powers with himself, a knight whomsoever he may choose to appoint, as judge of the law. And when such a dictator or master of the people is created, the other magistrates shall be suppressed...

Let the commanders, generals, and lieutenants, leave the city whenever the senate decrees or the people order that they shall do so. Let them properly prosecute all just wars. Let them spare our allies and restrain themselves and their subordinates. Let them increase the glory of our country. Let them return home with honor. Let no one be made an ambassador with a view to his own interest.

Let the ten officers whom the people elect to protect them against oppression be their tribunes, and let all their prohibitions and adjudications be established, and their persons considered inviolable, so that tribunes may never be wanting to the people.

Let all magistrates possess their auspices and jurisdictions, and let the senate be composed of these legitimate authorities. Let its ordinances be absolute and let its enactments be written and ratified, unless an equal or greater authority disagrees with them. Let the order of the senators be free from reproach and scandal and let them be an example of virtue to all...

If any question occurs out of the established jurisdiction of the magistrates, let another magistrate be appointed by the people, whose jurisdiction shall expressly extend thereto. Let the consul, the praetor, the censor, the master of the people and he to whom the senate has committed the election of consuls, have full liberty to treat both with the senate and the people, and endeavor to reconcile the interests of all parties. Let the tribunes of the people likewise have free access to the senate and advocate the interests of the people in all their deliberations. Let a just moderation predominate in the opinions and declarations of those who would thus act as mediators between the senate and the people. Let a senator who does not attend the senate either show cause of his non-attendance or submit to an appropriate fine. Let a senator speak in his turn, with all moderation, and let him be thoroughly acquainted with the interests of the people.

By all means avoid violence among the people. Let the greatest authority have the greatest weight in decisions. If any one shall disturb the public harmony and foment party quarrels, let him be punished as a criminal. To act the intercessor in cases of offence should be considered the part of a good citizen. Let those who act observe the auspices, obey the public augur, and carry into effect all proclamations, taking care that they are exhibited in the treasury and generally known. Let the public consultations be concentrated in one point at a time, let them instruct the people in the nature of the question, and let all the magistrates and the people be permitted to advise on the subject.

Let them permit no monopolies or privileges. With respect to the capital punishment of any citizen, let it not take place unless by the adjudication of the high courts of justice and the ministry of those whom the censors have placed over the popular orders. Let no bribes be given or received either in soliciting, discharging, or resigning an official situation.

If any one infringe upon any of these laws, let him be liable to penalty. Let these regulations be committed to the charge of the censors. Let public officers, on their retiring from their posts, give the censors an account of their conduct, but let them not by this means escape from legal prosecution if they have been guilty of corruption.

I have here recited the whole law; now, consider the question, and give your votes.

QUESTIONS FOR THOUGHT / DISCUSSION:

➢ Cicero states early in this discourse that a state without law is not a state at all. Why does he think that? Is law truly that important to the operation of a state?
➢ He also speaks of the magistrates—what we would call judges—and of the need to have an appeals process. Does he not trust the magistrates to do their job fairly and accurately?
➢ What makes the 'rule of law' beneficial to society? How does this provide the greatest good for the greatest number?

VII. John Stuart Mill: On Representative Government

John Stuart Mill (1806-1873) was an English philosopher and Member of Parliament who pursued a course of study throughout his life that included politics, economics, mathematics, history, and law. He was follower of Jeremy Bentham and the principles of Utilitarianism. It was his father, Scott James Mill, who educated him and originally introduced him to this philosophy, and planted the ideas that he would later use to reform the utilitarian ideology.

While John Stuart Mill continued to believe in the basic utilitarian idea that dictated people will do that which increases pleasure and avoids pain, he refined that philosophy somewhat by addressing the need to consider individual personalities and the human spirit. He believed that spiritual and emotional pleasure was as sought after by individuals as physical pleasure. Additionally, society as a whole has the need to increase the collective pleasure of the people and avoid the collective pain of the people. In short, society strives for the greatest good for the greatest number.

Mill also broke somewhat from the Benthamites by distinguishing different qualities of pleasure. People did not just seek to maximize pleasure for its own sake, but to maximize some pleasures more than others. These pleasures that have higher values tend to be the intellectual pleasures.

Mill considered that the responsibility of government was to increase the quality of life of its people. He believed that in order to achieve this, the people must participate actively in government. In a small government system, such as a city or town, a direct type of democracy would work, while in a larger system, such as a nation-state, a representative type of democracy might be required.

However, when observing America's representative government, Mill agreed with Toqueville that this system had the potential to concern itself only with the will of the majority at any given time and not pay attention to the needs of the minority. For this reason he preferred a representative system of government that would allow a more professional class of people to make decisions, while the people still retained the ultimate sovereignty.

The following excerpts were taken from Mill's Considerations on Representative Government, Chapter I and Chapter VII.

J.S. Mill: Representative Government

Forms of Government are a Matter of Choice

All speculations concerning forms of government bear the impress, more or less exclusive, of two conflicting theories respecting political institutions; or, to speak more properly, conflicting conceptions of what political institutions are.

By some minds, government is conceived as strictly a practical art, giving rise to no questions but those of means and an end. Forms of government are assimilated to any other expedients for the attainment of human objects. They are regarded as wholly an affair of invention and contrivance. Being made by man, it is assumed that man has the choice either to make them or not, and how or on what pattern they shall be made. Government, according to this conception, is a problem, to be worked like any other question of business. The first step is to define the purposes which governments are required to promote. The next, is to inquire what form of government is best fitted to fulfill those purposes.

Having satisfied ourselves on these two points, and ascertained the form of government which combines the greatest amount of good with the least of evil, what further remains is to obtain the concurrence of our countrymen, or those for whom the institutions are intended, in the opinion which we have privately arrived at. To find the best form of government, to persuade others that it is the best, and having done so, to stir them up to insist on having it, is the order of ideas in the minds of those who adopt this view of political philosophy. They look upon a constitution in the same light...as they would upon a steam plough, or a threshing machine.

To these stand opposed another kind of political reasoners, who are so far from assimilating a form of government to a machine, that they regard it as a sort of spontaneous product, and the science of government as a branch, so to speak, of natural history. According to them, forms of government are not a matter of choice. We must take them, in the main, as we find them. Governments cannot be constructed by premeditated design. They are "not made, but grown." Our business with them, as with the other facts of the universe, is to acquaint ourselves with their natural properties, and adapt ourselves to them. The fundamental political institutions of a people are considered by this school as a sort of organic growth from the nature and life of that people: a product of their habits, instincts, and unconscious wants and desires...

It is difficult to decide which of these doctrines would be the most absurd, if we could suppose either of them held as an exclusive theory. But the principles which men profess on any controverted subject, are usually a very incomplete exponent of the opinions they really hold. No one believes that every people is capable of working every sort of institutions... On the other hand, neither are those who speak of institutions as if they were a kind of living organisms really the political fatalists they give themselves out to be... But though each side greatly exaggerates its own theory, out of opposition to the other, and no one holds without modification to either, the two doctrines correspond to a deep-seated difference between two modes of thought; and though it is evident that neither of these is entirely in the right, yet it being equally evident that neither is wholly in the wrong, we must endeavor to get down to what is at the root of each, and avail ourselves of the amount of truth which exists in either.

Let us remember, then, in the first place, that political institutions...are the work of men, owe their origin and their whole existence to human will. Men did not wake on a summer morning and find them sprung up... In every stage of their existence they are made what they are by human voluntary agency. Like all things, therefore, which are made by men, they may be either well or ill made; judgment and skill may have been exercised in their production, or the reverse of these. And again, if a people have omitted, or from outward pressure have not had it in their power to give themselves a constitution by the tentative process of applying a corrective to each evil as it arose, or as the sufferers gained strength to resist it, this retardation of political progress is no doubt a great disadvantage to them, but it does not prove that what has been found good for others would not have been good also for them, and will not be so still when they think fit to adopt it.

On the other hand, it is also to be borne in mind that political machinery does not act of itself. As it is first made, so it has to be worked by men, and even by ordinary men. It needs not their simple acquiescence, but their active participation, and must be adjusted to the capacities and qualities of such men as are available. This implies three conditions. The people for whom the form of government is intended must be willing to accept it, or at least not so unwilling as to pose an insurmountable obstacle to its establishment. They must be willing and able to do what is necessary to keep it standing. And they must be willing and able to do what it requires of them to enable it to fulfill its purposes. The word 'do' is to be understood as including forbearances as well as acts. They must be capable of fulfilling the conditions of action and the conditions of self-restraint, which are necessary either for keeping the established polity in existence, or for enabling it to achieve the ends...The failure of any of these conditions renders a form of government, whatever favorable promise it may otherwise hold out, unsuitable to the particular case.

The first obstacle, the repugnance of the people to the particular form of government, needs little illustration, because it never can in theory have been overlooked. The case is of perpetual occurrence... There are nations who will not voluntarily submit to any government but that of certain families, which have from time immemorial had the privilege of supplying them with chiefs. Some nations could not, except by foreign conquest, be made to endure a monarchy; others are equally averse to a republic. The hindrance often amounts, for the time being, to impracticability.

But there are also cases in which, though not averse to a form of government...a people may be unwilling or unable to fulfill its conditions. They may be incapable of fulfilling such of them as are necessary to keep the government even in nominal existence. Thus a people may prefer a free government, but if, from indolence or carelessness or cowardice or want of public spirit, they are unequal to the exertions necessary for preserving it; if they will not fight for it when it is directly attacked, if they can be deluded by the artifices used to cheat them out of it; if by momentary discouragement, or temporary panic, or a fit of enthusiasm for an individual, they can be induced to lay their liberties at the feet even of a great man, or trust him with powers which enable him to subvert their institutions; in all these cases they are more or less unfit for liberty: and though it may be for their good to have had it even for a short time, they are unlikely long to enjoy it. Again, a people may be unwilling or unable to fulfill the duties which a particular form of government requires of them.

A rude people, though in some degree alive to the benefits of civilized society, may be unable to practice the forbearance which it demands: their passions may be too violent, or their personal pride too exacting, to forego private conflict, and leave to the laws the avenging of their real or supposed wrongs. In such a case, a civilized government, to be really advantageous to them, will require to be in a considerable degree despotic: to be one over which they do not themselves exercise control, and which imposes a great amount of forcible restraint upon their actions. Again, a people must be considered unfit for more than a limited and qualified freedom, who will not cooperate actively with the law and the public authorities in the repression of evildoers. A people who...are revolted by an execution, but not shocked at an assassination—require that the public authorities should be armed with much sterner powers of repression than elsewhere, since the first indispensable requisites of civilized life have nothing else to rest on.

These deplorable states of feeling, in any people who have emerged from savage life are, no doubt, usually the consequence of previous bad government, which has taught them to regard the law as made for other ends than their good, and its administrators as worse enemies than those who openly violate it. But however little blame may be due to those in whom these mental habits have grown up, and however the habits may be ultimately conquerable by better government, yet while they exist a people so disposed cannot be governed with as little power exercised over them as a people whose sympathies are on the side of the law, and who are willing to give active assistance in its enforcement. Again, representative institutions are of little value, and may be a mere instrument of tyranny or intrigue, when the generality of electors are not sufficiently interested in their own government to give their vote, or, if they vote at all, do not bestow their suffrages on public grounds, but sell them for money, or vote at the beck of some one who has control over them, or whom for private reasons they desire to propitiate. Popular election thus practiced, instead of a security against misgovernment, is but an additional wheel in its machinery.

Besides these moral hindrances, mechanical difficulties are often an insuperable impediment to forms of government. In the ancient world, though there might be, and often was, great individual or local independence, there could be nothing like a regulated popular government beyond the bounds of a single city-community; because there did not exist the physical conditions for the formation and propagation of a public opinion, except among those who could be brought together to discuss public matters in the same arena. This obstacle is generally thought to have ceased by the adoption of the representative system...

We have now examined the three fundamental conditions of the adaptation of forms of government to the people who are to be governed by them. ...When an institution, or a set of institutions, has the way prepared for it by the opinions, tastes, and habits of the people, they are not only more easily induced to accept it, but will more easily learn and will be, from the beginning, better disposed to do what is required of them both for the preservation of the institutions, and for bringing them into such action as enables them to produce their best results. It would be a great mistake in any legislator not to shape his measures so as to take advantage of such pre-existing habits and feelings when available.

On the other hand, it is an exaggeration to elevate these mere aids and facilities into necessary conditions. People are more easily induced to do, and do more easily, what they are already used to; but people also learn to do things new to them. Familiarity is a great help; but much dwelling on an idea will make it familiar, even when strange at first. There are abundant instances in which a whole people have been eager for untried things. The amount of capacity which a people possess for doing new things, and adapting themselves to new circumstances, is itself one of the elements of the question...

To recommend and advocate a particular institution or form of government, and set its advantages in the strongest light, is one of the modes, often the only mode within reach, of educating the mind of the nation not only for accepting or claiming, but also for working, the institution...Those, however, who undertake such a task, need to be duly impressed, not solely with the benefits of the institution or polity which they recommend, but also with the capacities, moral, intellectual, and active, required for working it, that they may avoid, if possible, stirring up a desire too much in advance of the capacity.

The result of what has been said is that, within the limits set by the three conditions so often adverted to, institutions and forms of government are a matter of choice. To inquire into the best form of government in the abstract...is not a chimerical, but a highly practical employment of scientific intellect; and to introduce into any country the best institutions which, in the existing state of that country, are capable of, in any tolerable degree, fulfilling the conditions, is one of the most rational objects to which practical effort can address itself. Everything which can be said by way of disparaging the efficacy of human will and purpose in matters of government might be said of it in every other of its applications. In all things there are very strict limits to human power. It can only act by wielding some one or more of the forces of nature. Forces, therefore, that can be applied to the desired use must exist; and will only act according to their own laws. We cannot make the river run backwards... In politics, as in mechanics, the power which is to keep the engine going must be sought for outside the machinery; and if it is not forthcoming, or is insufficient to surmount the obstacles which may reasonably be expected, the contrivance will fail. This is no peculiarity of the political art, and amounts only to saying that it is subject to the same limitations and conditions as all other arts.

At this point we are met by another objection, or the same objection in a different form. The forces, it is contended, on which the greater political phenomena depend, are not amenable to the direction of politicians or philosophers. The government of a country, it is affirmed, is, in all substantial respects, fixed and determined beforehand by the state of the country in regard to the distribution of the elements of social power. Whatever is the strongest power in society will obtain the governing authority; and a change in the political constitution cannot be durable unless preceded or accompanied by an altered distribution of power in society itself. A nation, therefore, cannot choose its form of government. The mere details and practical organization it may choose; but the essence of the whole, the seat of the supreme power, is determined for it by social circumstances.

That there is a portion of truth in this doctrine I at once admit; but to make it of any use, it must be reduced to a distinct expression and proper limits. When it is said that the strongest power in society will make itself strongest in the government, what is meant by power? ...To mere muscular strength, add two other elements, property and intelligence, and we are nearer the truth, but far from having yet reached it. Not only is a greater number often kept down by a lesser, but the greater number may have a preponderance in property, and individually in intelligence, and may yet be held in subjection, forcibly or otherwise, by a minority in both respects inferior to it. To make these various elements of power politically influential they must be organized; and the advantage in organization is necessarily with those who are in possession of the government. A much weaker party in all other elements of power may greatly preponderate when the powers of government are thrown into the scale; and may long retain its predominance through this alone: though, no doubt, a government so situated is in the condition called in mechanics unstable equilibrium, like a thing balanced on its smaller end which, if once disturbed, tends more and more to depart from, instead of reverting to, its previous state.

But there are still stronger objections to this theory of government in the terms in which it is usually stated. The power in society which has any tendency to convert itself into political power is...active power; in other words, power actually exerted... To think that because those who wield the power in society wield in the end that of government, therefore it is of no use to attempt to influence the constitution of the government by acting on opinion, is to forget that opinion is itself one of the greatest active social forces. One person with a belief is a social power equal to ninety-nine who have only interests. They who can succeed in creating a general persuasion that a certain form of government, or social fact of any kind, deserves to be preferred, have made nearly the most important step which can possibly be taken towards ranging the powers of society on its side... The serfs in Russia owe their emancipation, if not to a sentiment of duty, at least to the growth of a more enlightened opinion respecting the true interest of the State. It is what men think that determines how they act; and though the persuasions and convictions of average men are in a much greater degree determined by their personal position than by reason, no little power is exercised over them by the persuasions and convictions of those whose personal position is different, and by the united authority of the instructed.

When, therefore, the instructed in general can be brought to recognize one social arrangement, or political or other institution, as good, and another as bad, one as desirable, another as condemnable, very much has been done towards giving to the one, or withdrawing from the other, that preponderance of social force which enables it to subsist. And the maxim, that the government of a country is what the social forces in existence compel it to be, is true only in the sense in which it favors, instead of discouraging, the attempt to exercise, among all forms of government practicable in the existing condition of society, a rational choice.

Representation of All and of the Majority Only

It has been seen that the dangers incident to a representative democracy are of two kinds: danger of a low grade of intelligence in the representative body and in the popular opinion which controls it; and danger of class legislation on the part of the numerical majority, these being all composed of the same class. We have next to consider how far it is possible so to organize the democracy, without interfering materially with the characteristic benefits of democratic government, to do away with these two great evils, or at least to abate them, in the utmost degree attainable by human contrivance.

The common mode of attempting this is by limiting the democratic character of the representation, through a more or less restricted suffrage. But there is a previous consideration which, duly kept in view, considerably modifies the circumstances which are supposed to render such a restriction necessary. A completely equal democracy, in a nation in which a single class composes the numerical majority, cannot be divested of certain evils; but those evils are greatly aggravated by the fact that the democracies, which at present exist, are not equal but systematically unequal in favor of the predominant class.

Two very different ideas are usually confounded under the name democracy. The pure idea of democracy, according to its definition, is the government of the whole people by the whole people, equally represented. Democracy, as commonly conceived and hitherto practiced, is the government of the whole people by a mere majority of the people, exclusively represented. The former is synonymous with the equality of all citizens; the latter, strangely confounded with it, is a government of privilege, in favor of the numerical majority, who alone possess practically any voice in the State. This is the inevitable consequence of the manner in which the votes are now taken, to the complete disfranchisement of minorities.

The confusion of ideas here is great, but it is so easily cleared up that one would suppose the slightest indication would be sufficient to place the matter in its true light before any mind of average intelligence. It would be so, but for the power of habit, owing to which the simplest idea, if unfamiliar, has as great difficulty in making its way to the mind as a far more complicated one. That the minority must yield to the majority, the smaller number to the greater, is a familiar idea; and accordingly men think there is no necessity for using their minds any further, and it does not occur to them that there is any medium between allowing the smaller number to be equally powerful with the greater, and blotting out the smaller number altogether. In a representative body actually deliberating, the minority must of course be overruled; and in an equal democracy (since the opinions of the constituents, when they insist on them, determine those of the representative body) the majority of the people, through their representatives, will outvote and prevail over the minority and their representatives.

But does it follow that the minority should have no representatives at all? Because the majority ought to prevail over the minority, must the majority have all the votes, the minority none? Is it necessary that the minority should not even be heard? Nothing but habit and old association can reconcile any reasonable being to the needless injustice. In a truly equal democracy, every section would be represented, not disproportionately, but proportionately. A majority of the electors would always have a majority of the representatives; but a minority of the electors would always have a minority of the representatives. Man for man they would be as fully represented as the majority. Unless they are, there is not equal government, but a government of inequality and privilege; one part of the people rule over the rest. There is a part whose fair and equal share of influence in the representation is withheld from them, contrary to all just government, but above all, contrary to the principle of democracy, which professes equality as its very root and foundation.

The injustice and violation of principle are not less flagrant because those who suffer by them are a minority; for there is not equal suffrage where every single individual does not count for as much as any other single individual in the community. But it is not only a minority who suffer. Democracy, thus constituted, does not even attain its ostensible object, that of giving the powers of government in all cases to the numerical majority. It does something very different: it gives them to a majority of the majority; who may be, and often are, but a minority of the whole.

All principles are most effectually tested by extreme cases. Suppose then, that in a country governed by equal and universal suffrage, there is a contested election in every constituency, and every election is carried by a small majority. The Parliament thus brought together represents little more than a bare majority of the people. This Parliament proceeds to legislate, and adopts important measures by a bare majority of itself. What guarantee is there that these measures accord with the wishes of a majority of the people? Nearly half the electors, having been outvoted at the hustings, have had no influence at all in the decision; and the whole of these may be, a majority of them probably are, hostile to the measures, having voted against those by whom they have been carried. Of the remaining electors, nearly half have chosen representatives who, by supposition, have voted against the measures. It is possible, therefore, and not at all improbable, that the opinion which has prevailed was agreeable only to a minority of the nation, though a majority of that portion of it whom the institutions of the country have erected into a ruling class. If democracy means the certain ascendancy of the majority, there are no means of insuring that but by allowing every individual figure to tell equally in the summing up. Any minority left out, either purposely or by the play of the machinery, gives the power not to the majority, but to a minority in some other part of the scale.

The only answer which can possibly be made to this reasoning is, that as different opinions predominate in different localities, the opinion which is in a minority in some places has a majority in others, and on the whole every opinion which exists in the constituencies obtains its fair share of voices in the representation. And this is roughly true in the present state of the constituency; if it were not, the discordance of the House with the general sentiment of the country would soon become evident. But it would be no longer true if the present constituency were much enlarged; still less, if made co-extensive with the whole population; for in that case the majority in every locality would consist of manual laborers; and when there was any question pending, on which these classes were at issue with the rest of the community, no other class could succeed in getting represented anywhere. Even now, is it not a great grievance that in every Parliament a very numerous portion of the electors, willing and anxious to be represented, have no member in the House for whom they have voted?...

The constituencies to which most of the highly educated and public spirited persons in the country belong, those of the large towns, are now, in great part, either unrepresented or misrepresented. The electors who are on a different side in party politics from the local majority are unrepresented. Of those who are on the same side, a large proportion are misrepresented, having been obliged to accept the man who had the greatest number of supporters in their political party, though his opinions may differ from theirs on every other point. The state of things is, in some respects, even worse than if the minority were not allowed to vote at all; for then, at least, the majority might have a member who would represent their own best mind, while now, the necessity of not dividing the party, for fear of letting in its opponents, induces all to vote either for the first person who presents himself wearing their colors, or for the one brought forward by their local leaders; and these, if we pay them the compliment, which they very seldom deserve, of supposing their choice to be unbiased by their personal interests, are compelled, that they may be sure of mustering their whole strength, to bring forward a candidate whom none of the party will strongly object to—that is, a man without any distinctive peculiarity, any known opinions except the shibboleth of the party.

This is strikingly exemplified in the United States, where, at the election of President, the strongest party never dares put forward any of its strongest men, because every one of these, from the mere fact that he has been long in the public eye, has made himself objectionable to some portion or other of the party, and is therefore not so sure a card for rallying all their votes as a person who has never been heard of by the public at all until he is produced as the candidate. Thus, the man who is chosen, even by the strongest party, represents perhaps the real wishes only of the narrow margin by which that party outnumbers the other. Any section whose support is necessary to success possesses a veto on the candidate. Any section, which holds out more obstinately than the rest, can compel all the others to adopt its nominee; and this superior pertinacity is unhappily more likely to be found among those who are holding out for their own interest than for that of the public. The choice of the majority is therefore very likely to be determined by that portion of the body who are the most timid, the most narrow minded and prejudiced, or who cling most tenaciously to the exclusive class interest; in which case the electoral rights of the minority, while useless for the purposes for which votes are given, serve only for compelling the majority to accept the candidate of the weakest or worst portion of themselves.

That, while recognizing these evils, many should consider them as the necessary price paid for a free government is in no way surprising; it was the opinion of all the friends of freedom up to a recent period. But the habit of passing them over as irremediable has become so inveterate that many persons seem to have lost the capacity of looking at them as things which they would be glad to remedy if they could. From despairing of a cure, there is too often but one step to denying the disease; and from this follows dislike to having a remedy proposed, as if the proposer were creating a mischief instead of offering relief from one. People are so inured to the evils that they feel as if it were unreasonable, if not wrong, to complain of them. Yet, avoidable or not, he must be a purblind lover of liberty on whose mind they do not weigh; who would not rejoice at the discovery that they could be dispensed with. Now, nothing is more certain than that the virtual blotting out of the minority is no necessary or natural consequence of freedom; that, far from having any connection with democracy, it is diametrically opposed to the first principle of democracy, representation in proportion to numbers. It is an essential part of democracy that minorities should be adequately represented. No real democracy, nothing but a false show of democracy, is possible without it...

The natural tendency of representative government, as of modern civilization, is towards collective mediocrity: and this tendency is increased by all reductions and extensions of the franchise, their effect being to place the principal power in the hands of classes more and more below the highest level of instruction in the community. But though the superior intellects and characters will necessarily be outnumbered, it makes a great difference whether or not they are heard. In the false democracy, which, instead of giving representation to all gives it only to the local majorities, the voice of the instructed minority may have no organs at all in the representative body. It is an admitted fact that in the American democracy, which is constructed on this faulty model, the highly cultivated members of the community, except such of them as are willing to sacrifice their own opinions and modes of judgment, and become the servile mouthpieces of their inferiors in knowledge, seldom even offer themselves for Congress or the State Legislatures, so little likelihood have they of being returned. ...

The minority of instructed minds scattered through the local constituencies would unite to return a number, proportioned to their own numbers, of the very ablest men the country contains. They would be under the strongest inducement to choose such men, since in no other mode could they make their small numerical strength tell for anything considerable. The representatives of the majority, besides that they would themselves be improved in quality by the operation of the system, would no longer have the whole field to themselves. They would indeed outnumber the others, as much as the one class of electors outnumbers the other in the country: they could always out vote them, but they would speak and vote in their presence, and subject to their criticism. When any difference arose, they would have to meet the arguments of the instructed few by reasons, at least apparently, as cogent; and since they could not, as those do who are speaking to persons already unanimous, simply assume that they are in the right, it would occasionally happen to them to become convinced that they were in the wrong. As they would in general be well-meaning (for thus much may reasonably be expected from a fairly chosen national representation), their own minds would be insensibly raised by the influence of the minds with which they were in contact, or even in conflict.

The champions of unpopular doctrines would not put forth their arguments merely in books and periodicals, read only by their own side; the opposing ranks would meet face to face and hand to hand, and there would be a fair comparison of their intellectual strength in the presence of the country. It would then be found out whether the opinion which prevailed by counting votes, would also prevail if the votes were weighed as well as counted. The multitude has often a true instinct for distinguishing an able man, when he has the means of displaying his ability in a fair field before them. If such a man fails to obtain at least some portion of his just weight, it is through institutions or usages which keep him out of sight...

But if the presence in the representative assembly can be insured of even a few of the first minds in the country, though the remainder consist only of average minds, the influence of these leading spirits is sure to make itself sensibly felt in the general deliberations, even though they be known to be, in many respects, opposed to the tone of popular opinion and feeling...

This portion of the Assembly would also be the appropriate organ of a great social function, for which there is no provision in any existing democracy, but which in no government can remain permanently unfulfilled without condemning that government to infallible degeneracy and decay. This may be called the function of Antagonism. In every government there is some power stronger than all the rest; and the power which is strongest tends perpetually to become the sole power. Partly by intention, and partly unconsciously, it is ever striving to make all other things bend to itself; and is not content while there is anything which makes permanent head against it, any influence not in agreement with its spirit. Yet if it succeeds in suppressing all rival influences and molding everything after its own model, improvement in that country is at an end and decline commences.

Human improvement is a product of many factors, and no power ever yet constituted among mankind includes them all. Even the most beneficent power only contains in itself some of the requisites of good, and the remainder, if progress is to continue, must be derived from some other source. No community has ever long continued progressive, but while a conflict was going on between the strongest power in the community and some rival power; between the spiritual and temporal authorities; the military or territorial and the industrious classes; the king and the people; the orthodox and religious reformers. When the victory on either side was so complete as to put an end to the strife, and no other conflict took its place, first stagnation followed, and then decay.

The ascendancy of the numerical majority is less unjust, and on the whole less mischievous, than many others, but it is attended with the very same kind of dangers, and even more certainly; for when the government is in the hands of One or a Few, the Many are always existent as a rival power, which may not be strong enough ever to control the other, but whose opinion and sentiment are a moral, and even a social support to all who, either from conviction or contrariety of interest, are opposed to any of the tendencies of the ruling authority. But when the Democracy is supreme, there is no One or Few strong enough for dissentient opinions and injured or menaced interests to lean upon...

Now, this great want the system of Personal Representation is fitted to supply in the most perfect manner, which the circumstances of modern society admit of. The only quarter in which to look for a supplement, or completing corrective, to the instincts of a democratic majority, is the instructed minority...

The instructed minority would, in the actual voting, count only for their numbers, but as a moral power they would count for much more, in virtue of their knowledge, and of the influence it would give them over the rest. An arrangement better adapted to keep popular opinion within reason and justice, and to guard it from the various deteriorating influences, which assail the weak side of democracy, could scarcely by human ingenuity be devised...

QUESTIONS FOR THOUGHT / DISCUSSION:

➤ Mill says at the beginning of this selection that he thinks men must find the government system that combines the most good with the least evil. Do you think he finds government to be inherently evil? If so, why have any government at all?

➤ Mill discusses here whether or not men have control over the type of government under which they live. Does he

believe men have a choice or does the system simply
evolve as needed over time depending on circumstances?
Which do you think happens?

➤ What does Mill have to say about rule by numerical
majorities and the impact this type of democracy has on
minorities?

IX. Horace Mann:
Report on the Public Schools

Horace Mann (1796-1859) was an early champion of public secular education for all children. He felt that having all of the population educated was the only way to have a truly democratic society. "The well-being of a community is to be estimated not so much by possessing a few men of great knowledge, as its having many men of competent knowledge." The only way to create a moral society of virtuous people who would strive for the common good, would be to have all of the people educated as a means of preventing many of society's ills from ever taking root—crime, poverty, drunkenness, violence, and assorted other vices. Enlightened people are morally virtuous members of society.

As Secretary of the Massachusetts Board of Education, Mann was instrumental in the improvement of teacher training with the founding of Normal Schools—teacher training schools run by the state government. He helped to start the public education system of Common Schools, designed to educate all children. He opposed corporal punishment in the schools and advocated non-religious education.

Education was not Mann's only concern; during his lifetime he was also active in the temperance movement and in the creation of state hospitals for the insane. He served ten years in the Massachusetts state legislature and in 1848 was elected to the U.S. House of Representatives to fill a vacancy left by the death of former president John Quincy Adams.

Horace Mann: Report On The Public Schools

I feel fully justified in affirming, that the prospects of the rising generation are daily growing brighter, by means of the increasing light which is shed upon them from our Common Schools. Stronger feelings and firmer convictions of the importance of our Common Schools are taking possession of the public mind, and where they have not yet manifested themselves in any outward and visible improvement, they are silently and gradually working to that end.

It must not, however, be inferred, that the most extensive reform is not still necessary in regard to those edifices, where the business of education, for the great mass of the children in the State, is carried on. Every other class of edifices, whether public or private, has felt the hand of reform. Churches, court-houses, even jails and prisons are rebuilt or remodeled, great regard being paid in most cases to ornament, and in all cases to health, to personal convenience and accommodation. But the schoolhouse, which leads directly towards the church, or rather may be considered as its vestibule, and which furnishes to the vast majority of our children the only public means they will ever enjoy for qualifying themselves to profit by its counsels, its promises, its warnings, its consolations— the schoolhouse, which leads directly from the courthouse, from the jail and from the prison, and is, for the mass of our children, the great preventive and safeguard against being called or forced into them, as litigants or as criminals—this class of buildings, all over the State, stands in afflicting contrast with all the others. The courthouses, which are planned and erected under the advice and control of the county authorities and of the leading men in the county for themselves and in which they spend but a few terms in the year, and the meeting houses, where the parents spend but a few hours in a week, are provided with costly embellishments and with every appurtenance that can gratify taste or comfort; but the houses where the children, in the most susceptible period of their lives, spend from thirty to forty hours in a week, seem to be deserted by all public care and abandoned to cheerlessness and dilapidation.

If, in a portion of the manufacturing districts in the State, a regular and systematic obedience is paid to the law, while in other places it is regularly and systematically disregarded, the inevitable consequences to the latter will be obvious, upon a moment's reflection. The neighborhood or town where the law is broken will soon become the receptacle of the poorest, most vicious and abandoned parents, who are bringing up their children to be also as poor, vicious and abandoned as themselves. The whole class of parents, who cannot obtain employment for their children at one place but are welcomed at another, will circulate through the body politic until at last they will settle down as permanent residents in the latter; like the vicious humors of the natural body, which, being thrown off by every healthy part, at last accumulate and settle upon a diseased spot. Every breach of this law, therefore, inflicts direct and positive injustice, not only upon the children employed, but upon all the industrious and honest communities in which they are employed; because its effect will be to fill those communities with paupers and criminals—or at least with a class of persons, who, without being absolute technical paupers, draw their subsistence in a thousand indirect ways from the neighborhood where they reside; and without being absolute criminals in the eye of the law, still commit a thousand injurious, predatory acts, more harassing and annoying to the peace and security of a village than many classes of positive crimes.

While waterpower only is used for manufacturing purposes, a natural limit is affixed in every place to the extension of manufactories. The power being all taken up in any place, the further investment of capital and the employment of an increased number of operatives must cease. While we restrict ourselves to the propulsion of machinery by water, therefore it is impossible that we should have such an extensive manufacturing district as, for instance, that of Manchester in England, because we have no streams of sufficient magnitude for the purpose. But Massachusetts is already the greatest manufacturing State in the Union. Her best sites are all taken up and yet her disposition to manufacture appears not to be checked. Under such circumstances it seems not improbable that steam power will be resorted to; and if steam is employed, there is no assignable limit to the amount of a manufacturing population that may be gathered into a single manufacturing district. If, therefore, we would not have in any subsequent time, a population like that of the immense city of Manchester, where great numbers of the laboring population live in the filthiest streets, and mostly in houses which are framed back to back, so that in no case is there any yard behind them, but all ingress and egress for all purposes is between the front side of the house and the public street—if we would not have such a population, we must not only have preventive laws, but we must see that no cupidity, no contempt of the public welfare for the sake of private gain is allowed openly to violate or clandestinely to evade them. It would, indeed, be most lamentable and self-contradictory if, with all our institutions devised and prepared on the hypothesis of common intelligence and virtue, we should rear a class of children to be set apart and, as it were, dedicated to ignorance and vice.

It is obvious that children of ten, twelve, or fourteen years of age may be steadily worked in our manufactories without any schooling, and that this cruel deprivation may be persevered in for six, eight, or ten years, and yet, during all this period, no very alarming outbreak shall occur to rouse the public mind from its guilty slumber. The children are in their years of minority and they have no control over their own time or their own actions. The bell is to them what the water wheel and the main shaft are to the machinery, which they superintend. The wheel revolves and the machinery must go; the bell rings and the children must assemble. In their hours of work they are under the police of the establishment; at other times they are under the police of the neighborhood.

Hence this state of things may continue for years and the peace of the neighborhood remains undisturbed, except, perhaps, by a few nocturnal or Sabbath Day depredations. The ordinary movements of society may go on without any shocks or collisions as, in the human system, a disease may work at the vitals and gain a fatal ascendancy there before it manifests itself on the surface. But the punishment for such an offence will not be remitted because its infliction is postponed. The retribution, indeed, is not postponed, it only awaits the full completion of the offence, for this is a crime of such magnitude that it requires years for the criminal to perpetrate it in and to finish it off thoroughly in all its parts. But when the children pass from the condition of restraint to that of freedom, from years of enforced but impatient servitude to that independence for which they have secretly pined, and to which they have looked forward not merely as the period of emancipation, but of long delayed indulgence— when they become strong in the passions and propensities that grow up spontaneously, but are weak in the moral powers that control them, and blind in the intellect which foresees their tendencies—when, according to the course of our political institutions, they go by one bound from the political nothingness of a child to the political sovereignty of a man, then for that people, who so cruelly neglected and injured them, there will assuredly come a day of retribution.

But by far the most important subject respecting which I have sought for information during the year remains to be noticed. While we are in little danger of overestimating the value of Common Schools, yet we shall err egregiously if we regard them as ends and not as means. A forgetfulness of this distinction would send the mass of our children of both sexes into the world scantily provided either with the ability or the disposition to perform even the most ordinary duties of life. Common Schools derive their value from the fact that they are an instrument more extensively applicable to the whole mass of the children than any other instrument ever yet devised. They are an instrument, by which the good men in society can send redeeming influences to those children who suffer under the calamity of vicious parentage and evil domestic associations. The world is full of lamentable proofs that the institution of the family may exist for an indefinite number of generations without mitigating the horrors of barbarism. But the institution of Common Schools is the offspring of an advanced state of civilization, and is incapable of coexisting with barbarian life, because should barbarism prevail, it would destroy the schools; should the schools prevail, they would destroy barbarism. They are the only civil institution capable of extending its beneficent arms to embrace and to cultivate in all parts of its nature, every child that comes into the world.

Young men, it may be said, have a larger circle of action; they can mingle more in a promiscuous society, at least they have a far wider range of business occupations, all of which stimulate thought, suggest inquiry and furnish means for improvement. But the sphere of females is domestic. Their life is comparatively secluded. The proper delicacy of the sex forbids them from appearing in the promiscuous marts of business, and even from mingling, as actors, in those less boisterous arenas where mind is the acting agent, as well an the object to be acted upon. If then, she is precluded from these sources of information and these incitements to inquiry by the unanimous and universal opinion of civilized nations, when she breaks away from comparative seclusion and retirement, she leaves her charms behind her; and if, at the same time she is debarred from access to books, by what means, through what channels, is she to obtain the knowledge so indispensable for the fit discharge of maternal and domestic duties, and for rendering herself an enlightened companion for intelligent men? Without books, except in cases of extraordinary natural endowment, she will be doomed to relative ignorance and incapacity.

The State, in its sovereign capacity has the deepest interest in this matter. If it would spread the means of intelligence and self-culture over its entire surface, making them diffusive as sunshine, causing them to penetrate into every hamlet and dwelling, and like the vernal sun, quickening into life the seeds of usefulness and worth wherever the prodigal hand of nature may have scattered them—it would call into existence an order of men who would establish a broader basis for its prosperity, and give a brighter luster to its name—who would improve its arts, impart wisdom to its counsels, and extend the beneficent sphere of its charities. Yet, not for its own sake only should it assume this work. It is a corollary from the axioms of its constitution that every child born within its borders shall be enlightened. Here are an inconceivable extent and magnitude of interests, sympathies, obligations—here are all the great instincts of humanity, working out their way to a greater or less measure of good, according to the light they enjoy—and, compared with this wide and deep mass of unrecorded life, all that emerges into history and is seen of man, is as nothing.

QUESTIONS FOR THOUGHT/DISCUSSION:

➤ In 1840 Horace Mann is talking about the need to educate women—something some people today might find interesting. Why does he consider this important and what would be the benefit to society in having women who are educated?

> In the beginning of this essay, Mann talks about the number of children working in the factories and the disadvantages of having them grow up there—in the factories—without the benefit of education. What does he think will be the result when these children reach adulthood?
> Why is it important for a democratic society to have an education system that is available to all children?

X. Adam Smith:
The Wealth of Nations

Adam Smith (1723-1790) was a Scottish philosopher and political economist whose book, An Inquiry into the Nature and Causes of the Wealth of Nations, which outlined his theories on economic liberalism, is thought of still today as the 'bible' of capitalism.

Smith believed that the economy needed to have a completely free reign without government interference of any kind. If people were free to pursue their own economic interests unfettered, they would maximize labor and resources to their advantage and the end result would be the betterment of all. This was what he termed the 'invisible hand' of the market; if individuals all work toward their own good, they will, as a matter of course, raise the living standard for everyone in society. We call this enlightened self-interest.

Smith defended the free market as the best instrument for the increase of wealth for individuals, societies, and nations. Along with the other natural law philosophies being advanced during the Enlightenment Era, he argued that there are natural laws at work in the economic realm, such as the laws of supply and demand, that would cause the free market to be self-regulating. Governments needed to take a hands-off (laissez-faire) approach to the economy because any interference would simply injure the natural process. John Stuart Mill read, and agreed with, Smith's Wealth of Nations. Karl Marx did not agree. A more modern follower of Smith's philosophy, Milton Friedman, has even opined that government involvement probably does more harm than good because it slows down the natural corrective process.

Although there are no governments left today that allow the market a completely free hand, we find different levels of government involvement ranging from capitalism to communism. Even the socialist systems that fall in the middle ranges offer a variety of economic systems depending on the amount of government involvement. In the following two

*passages from Smith's treatise on capitalism, he outlines the
disadvantages of governmental interference in two areas of the
economy: individual labor choices and trade among nations.*

Adam Smith: The Wealth Of Nations

The Principle of the Division of Labor

Thio divioion of labor, fiom which so many advantages are
derived, is not originally the effect of any human wisdom,
which foresees and intends that general opulence to which it
gives occasion. It is the necessary, though very slow and
gradual consequence of a certain propensity in human nature,
which has in view no such extensive utility—the propensity to
truck, barter, and exchange one thing for another.

Whether this propensity be one of those original
principles in human nature of which no further account can
be given; or whether, as seems more probable, it be the
necessary consequence of the faculties of reason and speech, it
belongs not to our present subject to inquire. It is common to
all men, and to be found in no other race of animals, which
seem to know neither this nor any other species of contracts.
Two greyhounds, in running down the same hare, have
sometimes the appearance of acting in some sort of concert.
Each turns her towards his companion, or endeavors to
intercept her when his companion turns her towards himself.
This, however, is not the effect of any contract, but of the
accidental concurrence of their passions in the same object at
that particular time. Nobody ever saw a dog make a fair and
deliberate exchange of one bone for another with another dog.
Nobody ever saw one animal by its gestures and natural cries
signify to another, this is mine, that yours; I am willing to
give this for that. When an animal wants to obtain something
either of a man or of another animal, it has no other means of
persuasion but to gain the favor of those whose service it
requires. A puppy fawns upon its dam, and a spaniel
endeavors by a thousand attractions to engage the attention
of its master who is at dinner, when it wants to be fed by him.

Man sometimes uses the same arts with his brethren, and
when he has no other means of engaging them to act
according to his inclinations, endeavors by every servile and

fawning attention to obtain their good will. He has not time, however, to do this upon every occasion. In civilized society he stands at all times in need of the cooperation and assistance of great multitudes, while his whole life is scarce sufficient to gain the friendship of a few persons. In almost every other race of animals each individual, when it is grown up to maturity, is entirely independent, and in its natural state has occasion for the assistance of no other living creature. But man has almost constant occasion for the help of his brethren, and it is in vain for him to expect it from their benevolence only. He will be more likely to prevail if he can interest their self-love in his favor, and show them that it is for their own advantage to do for him what he requires of them. Whoever offers to another a bargain of any kind, proposes to do this. Give me that which I want and you shall have this, which you want—is the meaning of every such offer; and it is in this manner that we obtain from one another the far greater part of those good offices which we stand in need of. It is not from the benevolence of the butcher, the brewer, or the baker that we expect our dinner, but from their regard to their own interest. We address ourselves, not to their humanity but to their self-love, and never talk to them of our own necessities but of their advantages.

Nobody but a beggar chooses to depend chiefly upon the benevolence of his fellow citizens. Even a beggar does not depend upon it entirely. The charity of well-disposed people, indeed, supplies him with the whole fund of his subsistence. But though this principle ultimately provides him with all the necessaries of life which he has occasion for, it neither does nor can provide him with them as he has occasion for them. The greater part of his occasional wants are supplied in the same manner as those of other people: by treaty, by barter, and by purchase. With the money which one man gives him he purchases food. The old clothes which another bestows upon him he exchanges for other old clothes which suit him better, or for lodging, or for food, or for money, with which he can buy either food, clothes, or lodging, as he has occasion.

As it is by treaty, by barter, and by purchase that we obtain from one another the greater part of those mutual good offices, which we stand in need of, so it is this same trucking disposition which originally gives occasion to the division of labor. In a tribe of hunters or shepherds a particular person makes bows and arrows, for example, with more readiness and dexterity than any other. He frequently exchanges them for cattle or for venison with his companions; and he finds at last that he can in this manner get more cattle and venison than if he himself went to the field to catch them. From a regard to his own interest, therefore, the making of bows and arrows grows to be his chief business, and he becomes a sort of armorer. Another excels in making the frames and covers of their little huts or movable houses. He is accustomed to be of use in this way to his neighbors, who reward him in the same manner with cattle and with venison, till at last he finds it his interest to dedicate himself entirely to this employment, and to become a sort of house carpenter. In the same manner a third becomes a smith or a brazier, a fourth a tanner or dresser of hides or skins, the principal part of the nothing of savages. And thus the certainty of being able to exchange all that surplus part of the produce of his own labor, which is over and above his own consumption, for such parts of the produce of other men's labor as he may have occasion for, encourages every man to apply himself to a particular occupation, and to cultivate and bring to perfection whatever talent or genius he may possess for that particular species of business.

The difference of natural talents in different men is, in reality, much less than we are aware of; and the very different genius which appears to distinguish men of different professions, when grown to maturity, is not upon many occasions so much the cause as the effect of the division of labor. The difference between the most dissimilar characters, between a philosopher and a common street porter, for example, seems to arise not so much from nature as from habit, custom, and education. When they came into the world, and for the first six or eight years of their existence, they were perhaps very much alike, and neither their parents nor playfellows could perceive any remarkable difference. About that age, or soon after, they come to be employed in very different occupations. The difference of talents comes then to be taken notice of, and widens by degrees, till at last the vanity of the philosopher is willing to acknowledge scarce any resemblance. But without the disposition to truck, barter, and exchange, every man must have procured to himself every necessary and convenience of life which he wanted. All must have had the same duties to perform, and the same work to do, and there could have been no such difference of employment as could alone give occasion to any great difference of talents.

As it is this disposition, which forms that difference of talents so remarkable among men of different professions, so it is this same disposition which renders that difference useful. Many tribes of animals acknowledged to be all of the same species derive from nature a much more remarkable distinction of genius than what, antecedent to custom and education, appears to take place among men. By nature a philosopher is not in genius and disposition half so different from a street porter, as a mastiff is from a greyhound, or a greyhound from a spaniel, or this last from a shepherd's dog. Those different tribes of animals, however, though all of the same species, are of scarce any use to one another. The strength of the mastiff is not, in the least, supported either by the swiftness of the greyhound, or by the sagacity of the spaniel, or by the docility of the shepherd's dog. The effects of those different geniuses and talents, for want of the power or disposition to barter and exchange, cannot be brought into a common stock, and do not in the least contribute to the better accommodation and convenience of the species. Each animal is still obliged to support and defend itself, separately and independently, and derives no sort of advantage from that variety of talents with which nature has distinguished its fellows.

Among men, on the contrary, the most dissimilar geniuses are of use to one another; the different produces of their respective talents, by the general disposition to truck, barter, and exchange, being brought, as it were, into a common stock where every man may purchase whatever part of the produce of other men's talents he has occasion for.

The Unreasonableness of Restraints

In the foregoing part of this chapter I have endeavored to show, even upon the principles of the commercial system, how unnecessary it is to lay extraordinary restraints upon the importation of goods from those countries with which the balance of trade is supposed to be disadvantageous.

Nothing, however, can be more absurd than this whole doctrine of the balance of trade, upon which not only these restraints but also almost all the other regulations of commerce are founded. When two places trade with one another, this doctrine supposes that if the balance is even, neither of them either loses or gains; but if it leans in any degree to one side, that one of them loses and the other gains in proportion to its declension from the exact equilibrium. Both suppositions are false. A trade, which is forced by means of bounties and monopolies, may be, and commonly is, disadvantageous to the country in whose favor it is meant to be established, as I shall endeavor to show hereafter. But that trade which, without force or constraint, is naturally and regularly carried on between any two places is always advantageous, though not always equally so, to both. By advantage or gain, I understand not the increase of the quantity of gold and silver, but that of the exchangeable value of the annual produce of the land and labor of the country, or the increase of the annual revenue of its inhabitants.

If the balance be even, and if the trade between the two places consist altogether in the exchange of their native commodities, they will, upon most occasions, not only both gain, but they will gain equally or very near equally; each will in this case afford a market for a part of the surplus produce of the other; each will replace a capital which had been employed in raising and preparing for the market this part of the surplus produce of the other, and which had been distributed among, and given revenue and maintenance to a certain number of its inhabitants. Some part of the inhabitants of each, therefore, will indirectly derive their revenue and maintenance from the other. As the commodities exchanged, too, are supposed to be of equal value, so the two capitals employed in the trade will, upon most occasions, be equal or very nearly equal; and both being employed in raising the native commodities of the two countries, the revenue and maintenance which their distribution will afford to the inhabitants of each will be equal or very nearly equal. This revenue and maintenance thus mutually afforded will be greater or smaller in proportion to the extent of their dealings. If these should annually amount to an hundred thousand pounds, for example, or to a million on each side, each of them would afford an annual revenue in the one case of an hundred thousand pounds, in the other of a million, to the inhabitants of the other.

If their trade should be of such a nature that one of them exported to the other nothing but native commodities, while the returns of that other consisted altogether in foreign goods, the balance in this case would still be supposed even, commodities being paid for with commodities. They would in this case too, both gain but they would not gain equally; and the inhabitants of the country which exported nothing but native commodities would derive the greatest revenue from the trade. If England, for example, should import from France nothing but the native commodities of that country and, not having such commodities of its own as were in demand there, should annually repay them by sending thither a large quantity of foreign goods, tobacco, we shall suppose, and East India goods—this trade, though it would give some revenue to the inhabitants of both countries, would give more to those of France than to those of England. The whole French capital annually employed in it would annually be distributed among the people of France. But that part of the English capital only which was employed in producing the English commodities with which those foreign goods were purchased would be annually distributed among the people of England. The greater part of it would replace the capitals which had been employed in Virginia, Indostan, and China, and which had given revenue and maintenance to those distant countries. If the capitals were equal or nearly equal, therefore, this employment of the French capital would augment much more the revenue of the people of France than that of the English capital would the revenue of the people of England. France would in this case carry on a direct foreign trade of consumption with England; whereas England would carry on a roundabout trade of the same kind with France. The different effects of a capital employed in the direct, and of one employed in the roundabout foreign trade of consumption have already been fully explained.

There is not, probably, between any two countries a trade which consists altogether in the exchange either of native commodities on both sides, or of native commodities on one side and of foreign goods on the other. Almost all countries exchange with one another partly native and partly foreign goods. That country, however, in whose cargoes there is the greatest proportion of native and the least of foreign goods, will always be the principal gainer.

If it was not with tobacco and East India goods but with gold and silver that England paid for the commodities annually imported from France, the balance in this case would be supposed uneven, commodities not being paid for with commodities, but with gold and silver. The trade, however, would, in this case as in the foregoing, give some revenue to the inhabitants of both countries, but more to those of France than to those of England. It would give some revenue to those of England. The capital which had been employed in producing the English goods that purchased this gold and silver, the capital which had been distributed among, and given revenue to certain inhabitants of England, would thereby be replaced and enabled to continue that employment. The whole capital of England would no more be diminished by this exportation of gold and silver than by the exportation of an equal value of any other goods. On the contrary, it would in most cases be augmented.

No goods are sent abroad but those for which the demand is supposed to be greater abroad than at home, and of which the returns consequently, it is expected, will be of more value at home than the commodities exported. If the tobacco, which in England is worth only a hundred thousand pounds, when sent to France will purchase wine, which is in England worth a hundred and ten thousand, this exchange will equally augment the capital of England by ten thousand pounds. If a hundred thousand pounds of English gold in the same manner purchase French wine, which in England is worth a hundred and ten thousand, this exchange will equally augment the capital of England by ten thousand pounds. As a merchant who has a hundred and ten thousand pounds worth of wine in his cellar is a richer man than he who has only a hundred thousand pounds worth of tobacco in his warehouse, so is he likewise a richer man than he who has only a hundred thousand pounds worth of gold in his coffers. He can put into motion a greater quantity of industry and give revenue, maintenance, and employment to a greater number of people than either of the other two. But the capital of the country is equal to the capitals of all its different inhabitants and the quantity of industry, which can be annually maintained in it, is equal to what all those different capitals can maintain. Both the capital of the country, therefore, and the quantity of industry which can be annually maintained in it, must generally be augmented by this exchange.

It would, indeed, be more advantageous for England that it could purchase the wines of France with its own hardware and broadcloth than with either the tobacco of Virginia or the gold and silver of Brazil and Peru. A direct foreign trade of consumption is always more advantageous than a roundabout one. But a roundabout foreign trade of consumption, which is carried on with gold and silver, does not seem to be less advantageous than any other equally roundabout one. Neither is a country which has no mines more likely to be exhausted of gold and silver by this annual exportation of those metals than one which does not grow tobacco by the like annual exportation of that plant. As a country which has wherewithal to buy tobacco will never be long in want of it, so neither will one be long in want of gold and silver which has wherewithal to purchase those metals.

It is a losing trade, it is said, which a workman carries on with the alehouse; and the trade which a manufacturing nation would naturally carry on with a wine country may be considered as a trade of the same nature. I answer that the trade with the alehouse is not necessarily a losing trade. In its own nature it is just as advantageous as any other, though perhaps somewhat more liable to be abused. The employment of a brewer and even that of a retailer of fermented liquors are as necessary divisions of labor as any other. It will generally be more advantageous for a workman to buy of the brewer the quantity he has occasion for than to brew it himself, and if he is a poor workman, it will generally be more advantageous for him to buy it by little and little of the retailer than a large quantity of the brewer. He may no doubt buy too much of either, as he may of any other dealers in his neighborhood—of the butcher, if he is a glutton, or of the draper, if he affects to be a beau among his companions.

It is advantageous to the great body of workmen, notwithstanding, that all these trades should be free, though this freedom may be abused in all of them, and is more likely to be so perhaps in some than in others. Though individuals, besides, may sometimes ruin their fortunes by an excessive consumption of fermented liquors, there seems to be no risk that a nation should do so. Though in every country there are many people who spend upon such liquors more than they can afford, there are always many more who spend less. It deserves to be remarked too, that if we consult experience, the cheapness of wine seems to be a cause not of drunkenness, but of sobriety. The inhabitants of the wine countries are in general the soberest people in Europe; witness the Spaniards, the Italians, and the inhabitants of the southern provinces of France. People are seldom guilty of excess in what is their daily fare. Nobody affects the character of liberality and good fellowship by being profuse of a liquor which is as cheap as small beer. On the contrary, in the countries which, either from excessive heat or cold produce no grapes, and where wine consequently is dear and a rarity, drunkenness is a common vice, as among the northern nations and all those who live between the tropics...

When a French regiment comes from some of the northern provinces of France where wine is somewhat dear, to be quartered in the southern where it is very cheap, the soldiers, I have frequently heard it observed, are at first debauched by the cheapness and novelty of good wine; but after a few months' residence, the greater part of them become as sober as the rest of the inhabitants. Were the duties upon foreign wines, and the excises upon malt, beer, and ale to be taken away all at once, it might, in the same manner, occasion in Great Britain a pretty general and temporary drunkenness among the middling and inferior ranks of people, which would probably be soon followed by a permanent and almost universal sobriety. At present drunkenness is by no means the vice of people of fashion, or of those who can easily afford the most expensive liquors. A gentleman drunk with ale has scarce ever been seen among us. The restraints upon the wine trade in Great Britain, besides, do not so much seem calculated to hinder the people from going, if I may say so, to the alehouse, as from going where they can buy the best and cheapest liquor. They favor the wine trade of Portugal and discourage that of France.

The Portuguese, it is said, indeed are better customers for our manufactures than the French, and should therefore be encouraged in preference to them. As they give us their custom, it is pretended, we should give them ours. The sneaking arts of underling tradesmen are thus erected into political maxims for the conduct of a great empire: for it is the most underling tradesmen only who make it a rule to employ chiefly their own customers. A great trader purchases his goods always where they are cheapest and best, without regard to any little interest of this kind.

By such maxims as these, however, nations have been taught that their interest consisted in beggaring all their neighbors. Each nation has been made to look with an invidious eye upon the prosperity of all the nations with which it trades, and to consider their gain as its own loss. Commerce, which ought naturally to be among nations as among individuals, a bond of union and friendship, has become the most fertile source of discord and animosity. The capricious ambition of kings and ministers has not, during the present and the preceding century, been more fatal to the repose of Europe than the impertinent jealousy of merchants and manufacturers. The violence and injustice of the rulers of mankind is an ancient evil, for which, I am afraid, the nature of human affairs can scarce admit of a remedy. But the mean rapacity, the monopolizing spirit of merchants and manufacturers, who neither are nor ought to be the rulers of mankind, though it cannot perhaps be corrected, may very easily be prevented from disturbing the tranquility of anybody but themselves.

That it was the spirit of monopoly, which originally both invented and propagated this doctrine, cannot be doubted; and they who first taught it were by no means such fools as they who believed it. In every country it always is and must be the interest of the great body of the people to buy whatever they want of those who sell it cheapest. The proposition is so very manifest that it seems ridiculous to take any pains to prove it; nor could it ever have been called in question had not the interested sophistry of merchants and manufacturers confounded the common sense of mankind. Their interest is, in this respect, directly opposite to that of the great body of the people. As it is the interest of the freemen of a corporation to hinder the rest of the inhabitants from employing any workmen but themselves, so it is the interest of the merchants and manufacturers of every country to secure to themselves the monopoly of the home market—hence, in Great Britain, and in most other European countries, the extraordinary duties upon almost all goods imported by alien merchants hence, the high duties and prohibitions upon all those foreign manufactures which can come into competition with our own. Hence, too, the extraordinary restraints upon the importation of almost all sorts of goods from those countries with which the balance of trade is supposed to be disadvantageous; that is, from those against whom national animosity happens to be most violently inflamed.

The wealth of a neighboring nation, however, though dangerous in war and politics, is certainly advantageous in trade. In a state of hostility it may enable our enemies to maintain fleets and armies superior to our own; but in a state of peace and commerce it must likewise enable them to exchange with us to a greater value and to afford a better market, either for the immediate produce of our own industry or for whatever is purchased with that produce. As a rich man is likely to be a better customer to the industrious people in his neighborhood than a poor, so is likewise a rich nation. A rich man, indeed, who is himself a manufacturer is a very dangerous neighbor to all those who deal in the same way. All the rest of the neighborhood, however, by far the greatest number, profit by the good market which his expense affords them. They even profit by his underselling the poorer workmen who deal in the same way with him. The manufacturers of a rich nation, in the same manner, may no doubt be very dangerous rivals to those of their neighbors.

This very competition, however, is advantageous to the great body of the people, who profit greatly besides by the good market, which the great expense of such a nation affords them in every other way. Private people who want to make a fortune never think of retiring to the remote and poor provinces of the country, but resort either to the capital or to some of the great commercial towns. They know that where little wealth circulates there is little to be got, but that where a great deal is in motion, some share of it may fall to them.

The same maxims, which would in this manner direct the common sense of one, or ten, or twenty individuals, should regulate the judgment of one, or ten, or twenty millions, and should make a whole nation regard the riches of its neighbors as a probable cause and occasion for itself to acquire riches. A nation that would enrich itself by foreign trade is certainly most likely to do so when its neighbors are all rich, industrious, and commercial nations. A great nation surrounded on all sides by wandering savages and poor barbarians might, no doubt, acquire riches by the cultivation of its own lands and by its own interior commerce, but not by foreign trade. It seems to have been in this manner that the ancient Egyptians and the modern Chinese acquired their great wealth. The ancient Egyptians, it is said, neglected foreign commerce, and the modern Chinese, it is known, hold it in the utmost contempt and scarce deign to afford it the decent protection of the laws. The modern maxims of foreign commerce, by aiming at the impoverishment of all our neighbors so far as they are capable of producing their intended effect, tend to render that very commerce insignificant and contemptible.

It is in consequence of these maxims that the commerce between France and England has in both countries been subjected to so many discouragements and restraints. If those two countries, however, were to consider their real interest without either mercantile jealousy or national animosity, the commerce of France might be more advantageous to Great Britain than that of any other country, and for the same reason that of Great Britain to France. France is the nearest neighbor to Great Britain. In the trade between the southern coast of England and the northern and northwestern coasts of France, the returns might be expected in the same manner as in the inland trade, four, five, or six times in the year. The capital, therefore, employed in this trade could in each of the two countries keep in motion four, five, or six times the quantity of industry and afford employment and subsistence to four, five, or six times the number of people, which an equal capital could do in the greater part of the other branches of foreign trade. Between the parts of France and

Great Britain most remote from one another, the returns
might be expected, at least once in the year, and even this
trade would so far be at least equally advantageous as the
greater part of the other branches of our foreign European
trade. It would be at least three times more advantageous
than the boasted trade with our North American colonies, in
which the returns were seldom made in less than three years,
frequently not in less than four or five years. France, besides,
is supposed to contain twenty-four millions of inhabitants.
Our North American colonies were never supposed to contain
more than three millions; and France is a much richer
country than North America; though, on account of the more
unequal distribution of riches, there is much more poverty
and beggary in the one country than in the other. France,
therefore, could afford a market at least eight times more
extensive and, on account of the superior frequency of the returns, four-and-twenty times more advantageous than that
which our North American colonies ever afforded.

The trade of Great Britain would be just as advantageous
to France and, in proportion to the wealth, population, and
proximity of the respective countries, would have the same
superiority over that which France carries on with her own
colonies. Such is the very great difference between that trade,
which the wisdom of both nations has thought proper to
discourage, and that which it has favored the most.

But the very same circumstances, which would have
rendered an open and free commerce between the two
countries so advantageous to both, have occasioned the
principal obstructions to that commerce. Being neighbors,
they are necessarily enemies, and the wealth and power of
each becomes, upon that account, more formidable to the
other; and what would increase the advantage of national
friendship serves only to inflame the violence of national
animosity. They are both rich and industrious nations; and
the merchants and manufacturers of each dread the competition of the skill and activity of those of the other.
Mercantile jealousy is excited, and both inflames and is itself
inflamed, by the violence of national animosity; and the
traders of both countries have announced with all the
passionate confidence of interested falsehood, the certain ruin
of each, in consequence of that unfavorable balance of trade,

which, they pretend, would be the infallible effect of an unrestrained commerce with the other.

There is no commercial country in Europe of which the approaching ruin has not frequently been foretold by the pretended doctors of this system from an unfavorable balance of trade. After all the anxiety, however, which they have excited about this, after all the vain attempts of almost all trading nations to turn that balance in their own favor and against their neighbors, it does not appear that any one nation in Europe has been in any respect impoverished by this cause. Every town and country, on the contrary, in proportion as they have opened their ports to all nations, instead of being ruined by this free trade, as the principles of the commercial system would lead us to expect, have been enriched by it. Though there are in Europe, indeed, a few towns, which in some respects deserve the name of free ports, there is no country which does so. Holland, perhaps, approaches the nearest to this character of any though still very remote from it; and Holland, it is acknowledged, not only derives its whole wealth, but a great part of its necessary subsistence, from foreign trade.

QUESTIONS FOR THOUGHT / DISCUSSION:

➤ What would happen if, instead of individuals deciding how they would labor and what they would specialize in, the government arbitrarily assigned roles and jobs to everyone?

➤ Smith compares the actions of rich men to that of rich nations. Why does Smith believe it is advantageous for a nation to be surrounded by rich nations?

➤ Smith uses two concepts in the above excerpts—the division of labor and specialization, and free trade among nations—to make his case for the greatest good. Do you agree with him that society will best be served by these actions?

XI. Karl Marx and Frederick Engels: The Communist Manifesto

Karl Marx (1818 1883) and Frederick Engels (1820-1895) were associates, friends, collaborators, philosophers, historians, and social scientists. Marx, the better known and probably more intelligent of the two, lent his name to the political ideology that would transform the world in the 20th century. He was born in Germany and studied law, history, and philosophy before settling in London, as a young adult, where he met Engels. Engels would serve as his sounding board and source of income for the rest of his life.

Marxism is a combination of ideas synthesized by Karl Marx into what has come to be seen as a world-renowned political ideology. The historical dialectic of the German philosopher Hegel is the basic premise. Here is the idea that all of history is a constant struggle that produces continuous change. We begin with a thesis that is challenged by opposition from within—its antithesis—and in turn produces a synthesis as the struggle is resolved. This new synthesis becomes its own new thesis, which will be challenged by an antithesis and form a new synthesis, and on and on. After a time there will eventually be no more struggles as each has been played out and resolved.

Marx saw most of the conflicts in society coming about as a result of economic concerns. Everyone's primary purpose is to provide for himself the basic necessities of life; how he provides these things determines the life he leads. In order to provide these things he must produce, and so he becomes dependent on the means of production to which he contributes his labor. This is how socioeconomic classes in society are created and how class struggles develop. Class struggles are the antitheses, which bring about change.

According to Marx, these class struggles would increase as the industrializing nations applied more and more technological innovations to the means of production, alienating and displacing the masses, who would eventually rise up against the capitalist owners of the means of production.

A selection from Marx's collaborative effort with Engels, the Communist Manifesto, is reproduced here. Some may find it odd that a political ideology that is in direct conflict with democracy would be included here. However, in theory, Marxism does advocate the greatest good for the greatest number. Marxism advocates ownership of all of society's resources by all members of society as a whole. If everything in a nation is combined and owned and shared communally, all would have the benefit of everything. Marx's problem is that he simply did not understand human nature or capitalism—or made a conscious effort to ignore some very basic principles concerning each.

Man may be a social animal but he is also an individual— and a selfish one at that. We do things that benefit ourselves. Many times this means benefiting society as well through enlightened self-interest. But we are, ultimately, trying to satisfy our own selfish desires. (See Jeremy Bentham and John Stuart Mill.)

Capitalism may be cold and cruel and exploitive, but it provides wealth and opportunities to gain wealth to people at all levels in society. It also uses resources most efficiently in order to maximize profits. The prosperity created by capitalism does not concentrate the wealth, as Marx supposed it would, but in fact, helps to spread the wealth so that all members of society benefit: 'A rising tide lifts all boats.'

Marx & Engels: The Communist Manifesto

A specter is haunting Europe—the specter of communism. All the powers of old Europe have entered into a holy alliance to exorcise this specter: Pope and Tsar...French Radicals and German police spies. Where is the party in opposition that has not been decried as communistic by its opponents in power? Where is the opposition that has not hurled back the branding reproach of communism, against the more advanced opposition parties, as well as against its reactionary adversaries? Two things result from this fact: Communism is already acknowledged by all European powers to be itself a power. It is high time that Communists should openly, in the face of the whole world, publish their views, their aims, their tendencies, and meet this nursery tale of the specter of communism with a manifesto of the party itself. To this end, Communists of various nationalities have assembled in London and sketched the following manifesto...

Bourgooioio and Prolotariano [6]

The history of all hitherto existing society is the history of class struggles. Freeman and slave, patrician and plebeian, lord and serf, guild-master and journeyman, in a word, oppressor and oppressed, stood in constant opposition to one another, carried on an uninterrupted, now hidden, now open fight, a fight that each time ended either in a revolutionary reconstitution of society at large or in the common ruin of the contending classes. In the earlier epochs of history, we find almost everywhere a complicated arrangement of society into various orders, a manifold gradation of social rank. In ancient Rome we have patricians, knights, plebeians, slaves; in the Middle Ages, feudal lords, vassals, guild-masters, journey-men, apprentices, serfs; in almost all of these classes, again, subordinate gradations. The modern bourgeois society that has sprouted from the ruins of feudal society has not done away with class antagonisms. It has but established new classes, new conditions of oppression, and new forms of struggle in place of the old ones.

Our epoch, the epoch of the bourgeoisie, possesses, however, this distinct feature: it has simplified class antagonisms. Society as a whole is more and more splitting up into two great hostile camps, into two great classes directly facing each other—bourgeoisie and proletariat. From the serfs of the Middle Ages sprang the chartered burghers of the earliest towns. From these burgesses the first elements of the bourgeoisie were developed. The discovery of America, the rounding of the Cape, opened up fresh ground for the rising bourgeoisie. The East Indian and Chinese markets, the colonization of America, trade with the colonies, the increase in the means of exchange and in commodities generally, gave

---

[6] Bourgeoisie means owners of production/capitalists; proletarians means workers/laborers.

to commerce, to navigation, to industry, an impulse never before known, and thereby, to the revolutionary element in the tottering feudal society, a rapid development.

The feudal system of industry, in which industrial production was monopolized by closed guilds,[7] now no longer suffices for the growing wants of the new markets. The manufacturing system took its place. The guild-masters were pushed aside by the manufacturing middle class; division of labor between the different corporate guilds vanished in the face of division of labor in each single workshop. Meantime, the markets kept ever growing, the demand ever rising. Even manufacturers no longer sufficed. Thereupon, steam and machinery revolutionized industrial production. The place of manufacture was taken by the modern industry, the place of the industrial middle class by industrial millionaires, the leaders of the whole industrial armies by the modern bourgeois.

Modern industry has established the world market, for which the discovery of America paved the way. This market has given an immense development to commerce, to navigation, to communication by land. This development has, in turn, reacted on the extension of industry; and in proportion as industry, commerce, navigation, railways extended, in the same proportion the bourgeoisie developed and increased its capital, and pushed into the background every class handed down from the Middle Ages.

We see, therefore, how the modern bourgeoisie is itself the product of a long course of development, of a series of revolutions in the modes of production and of exchange. Each step in the development of the bourgeoisie was accompanied by a corresponding political advance in that class...

The bourgeoisie has at last, since the establishment of modern industry and of the world market, conquered for itself, in the modern representative state, exclusive political sway...

The bourgeoisie has stripped of its halo every occupation hitherto honored and looked up to with reverent awe. It has converted the physician, the lawyer, the priest, the poet, and the man of science, into its paid wage laborers.

---

[7] Guilds are what we know as unions.

The bourgeoisie has torn away from the family its sentimental veil and has reduced the family relation into a mere money relation. The bourgeoisie has disclosed how it came to pass that the brutal display of vigor in the Middle Ages, which reactionaries so much admire, found its fitting complement in the most slothful indolence. It has been the first to show what man's activity can bring about. It has accomplished wonders far surpassing Egyptian pyramids, Roman aqueducts, and Gothic cathedrals; It has conducted expeditions that put in the shade all former exoduses of nations and crusades. The bourgeoisie cannot exist without constantly revolutionizing the instruments of production, and thereby the relations of production, and with them the whole relations of society...

All that is solid melts into air, all that is holy is profaned, and man is at last compelled to face with sober senses his real condition of life and his relations with his kind. The need of a constantly expanding market for its products chases the bourgeoisie over the entire surface of the globe. It must nestle everywhere, settle everywhere, establish connections everywhere.

The bourgeoisie has, through its exploitation of the world market, given a cosmopolitan character to production and consumption in every country. To the great chagrin of reactionaries, it has drawn from under the feet of industry the national ground on which it stood. All old established national industries have been destroyed or are daily being destroyed. They are dislodged by new industries, whose introduction becomes a life and death question for all civilized nations, by industries that no longer work up indigenous raw material, but raw material drawn from the remotest zones; industries whose products are consumed, not only at home, but in every quarter of the globe. In place of the old wants, satisfied by the production of the country, we find new wants, requiring for their satisfaction the products of distant lands and climes. In place of the old local and national seclusion and self-sufficiency, we have intercourse in every direction, universal interdependence of nations—and as in material, so also in intellectual production.

The intellectual creations of individual nations become common property. National one-sidedness and narrow mindedness become more and more impossible, and from the varieties of national and local literature, there arises a world literature.

The bourgeoisie, by the rapid improvement of all instruments of production, by the immensely facilitated means of communication, draws all, even the most barbarian nations into civilization. The cheap prices of commodities are the heavy artillery with which it forces the barbarians' intensely obstinate hatred of foreigners to capitulate. It compels all nations, on pain of extinction, to adopt the bourgeois mode of production; it compels them to introduce what it calls civilization into their midst, to become bourgeois themselves. In one word, it creates a world after its own image.

The bourgeoisie has subjected the country to the rule of the towns. It has created enormous cities, has greatly increased the urban population as compared with the rural, and has thus rescued a considerable part of the population from the idiocy of rural life. Just as it has made the country dependent on the towns, so it has made barbarian and semi-barbarian countries dependent on the civilized ones, nations of peasants on nations of bourgeois, the East on the West. The bourgeoisie keeps more and more doing away with the scattered state of the population, of the means of production, and of property. It has agglomerated population, centralized the means of production, and has concentrated property in a few hands. The necessary consequence of this was political centralization.

Independent, or loosely connected provinces, with separate interests, laws, governments, and systems of taxation, became lumped together into one nation, with one government, one code of laws, one national class interest, one frontier, and one customs tariff. The bourgeoisie, during its rule of barely one hundred years, has created more massive and more colossal productive forces than have all preceding generations together. Subjection of nature's forces to man, machinery, application of chemistry to industry and agriculture, steam navigation, railways, electric telegraphs, clearing of whole continents for cultivation, canals or rivers, whole populations conjured out of the ground—what earlier century had even a presentiment that such productive forces slumbered in the lap of social labor?...

In proportion as the bourgeoisie, the capital, is developed, in the same proportion is the proletariat, the modern working class, developed—a class of laborers who live only so long as they find work and who find work only so long as their labor increases capital. These laborers, who must sell themselves piecemeal, are a commodity, like every other article of commerce, and are consequently exposed to all the vicissitudes of competition, to all the fluctuations of the market.

Owing to the extensive use of machinery and to the division of labor, the work of the proletarians has lost all individual character and, consequently, all charm for the workman. He becomes an appendage of the machine and it is only the most simple, most monotonous, and most easily acquired knack that is required of him. Hence, the cost of production of a workman is restricted almost entirely to the means of subsistence that he requires for maintenance and for the propagation of his race. But the price of a commodity, and therefore also of labor, is equal to its cost of production. In proportion, therefore, as the repulsiveness of the work increases, the wage decreases. What is more, in proportion as the use of machinery and division of labor increases, in the same proportion the burden of toil also increases, whether by prolongation of the working hours, by the increase of the work exacted in a given time, or by increased speed of machinery, etc.

Modern industry has converted the little workshop of the patriarchal master into the great factory of the industrial capitalist. Masses of laborers, crowded into the factory, are organized like soldiers. As privates of the industrial army, they are placed under the command of a perfect hierarchy of officers and sergeants. Not only are they slaves of the bourgeois class and of the bourgeois state; they are daily and hourly enslaved by the machine, by the overseer, and above all, in the individual bourgeois manufacturer himself. The more openly this despotism proclaims gain to be its end and aim, the more petty, the more hateful, and the more embittering it is. The less the skill and exertion of strength implied in manual labor, in other words, the more modern industry becomes developed, the more is the labor of men superseded by that of women. Differences of age and sex have no longer any distinctive social validity for the working class. All are instruments of labor, more or less expensive. No sooner is the exploitation of the laborer by the manufacturer, so far at an end, that he receives his wages in cash, than he is set upon by the other portion of the bourgeoisie, the landlord, the shopkeeper, the pawnbroker, etc.

The lower strata of the middle class—the small tradesmen, shopkeepers, craftsmen, and peasants—all these sink gradually into the proletariat, partly because their diminutive capital does not suffice for the scale on which modern industry is carried on and is swamped in the competition with the large capitalists, partly because their specialized skill is rendered worthless by new methods of production. Thus, the proletariat is recruited from all classes of the population...

But with the development of industry, the proletariat not only increases in number; it becomes concentrated in greater masses, its strength grows, and it feels that strength more. The various interests and conditions of life within the ranks of the proletariat are more and more equalized, in proportion as machinery obliterates all distinctions of labor and nearly everywhere reduces wages to the same low level. The growing competition among the bourgeois, and the resulting commercial crises, make the wages of the workers ever more fluctuating. The increasing improvement of machinery, ever more rapidly developing, makes their livelihood more and more precarious; the collisions between individual workmen and individual bourgeois take more and more the character of collisions between two classes. Thereupon, the workers begin to form collectives (trade unions) against the bourgeois; they club together in order to keep up the rate of wages; they found permanent associations in order to make provision beforehand for these occasional revolts...

Of all the classes that stand face to face with the bourgeoisie today, the proletariat alone is a genuinely revolutionary class. The other classes decay and finally disappear in the face of modern industry; the proletariat is its special and essential product. The lower middle class, the small manufacturer, the shopkeeper, the artisan, the peasant —all these fight against the bourgeoisie, to save from extinction their existence as fractions of the middle class. They are therefore not revolutionary, but conservative. Indeed, they are reactionary, for they try to roll back the wheel of history. If, by chance, they are revolutionary, they are only so in view of their impending transfer into the proletariat; they thus defend not their present, but their future interests; they desert their own standpoint to place themselves at that of the proletariat...

The proletariat, the lowest stratum of our present society, cannot stir, cannot raise itself up without the whole superincumbent strata of official society being sprung into the air. Though not in substance, yet in form, the struggle of the proletariat with the bourgeoisie is at first a national struggle. The proletariat of each country must, first of all settle matters with its own bourgeoisie. In depicting the most general phases of the development of the proletariat, we traced the more or less veiled civil war, raging within existing society, up to the point where that war breaks out into open revolution, and where the violent overthrow of the bourgeoisie lays the foundation for the sway of the proletariat.

Hitherto, every form of society has been based, as we have already seen, on the antagonism of opprosssing and oppressed classes. But in order to oppress a class, certain conditions must be assured to it under which it can at least continue its slavish existence. The serf, in the period of serfdom, raised himself to membership in the commune, just as the petty bourgeois, under the yoke of the feudal absolutism, managed to develop into a bourgeois. The modern laborer, on the contrary, instead of rising with the process of industry, sinks deeper and deeper below the conditions of existence of his own class. He becomes a pauper and pauperism develops more rapidly than population and wealth. And here it becomes evident that the bourgeoisie is unfit any longer to be the ruling class in society, and to impose its conditions of existence upon society as an overriding law. It is unfit to rule because it is incompetent to assure an existence to its slave within his slavery, because it cannot help letting him sink into such a state, that it has to feed him, instead of being fed by him.

Society can no longer live under this bourgeoisie; in other words, its existence is no longer compatible with society. The essential conditions for the existence and for the sway of the bourgeois class is the formation and augmentation of capital; the condition for capital is wage labor. Wage labor rests exclusively on competition between the laborers. The advance of industry, whose involuntary promoter is the bourgeoisie, replaces the isolation of the laborers, due to competition, by the revolutionary combination, due to association. The development of modern industry, therefore, cuts from under its feet the very foundation on which the bourgeoisie produces and appropriates products. What the bourgeoisie therefore produces, above all, are its own gravediggers. Its fall and the victory of the proletariat are equally inevitable.

Proletarians and Communists

In what relation do the Communists stand to the proletarians as a whole? The Communists do not form a separate party opposed to the other working-class parties. They have no interests separate and apart from those of the proletariat as a whole. They do not set up any sectarian principles of their own, by which to shape and mould the proletarian movement. The Communists are distinguished from the other working-class parties by this only: 1. In the national struggles of the proletarians of the different countries, they point out and bring to the front the common interests of the entire proletariat, independently of all nationality. 2. In the various stages of development, which the struggle of the working class against the bourgeoisie has to pass through, they always and everywhere represent the interests of the movement as a whole. The Communists, therefore, are on the one hand practically the most advanced and resolute section of the working-class parties of every country, that section which pushes forward all others. On the other hand, theoretically, they have over the great mass of the proletariat the advantage of clearly understanding the direction, the conditions, and the ultimate general results of the proletarian movement.

The immediate aim of the Communists is the same as that of all other proletarian parties: formation of the proletariat into a class, overthrow of the bourgeois supremacy, and conquest of political power by the proletariat.

The theoretical conclusions of the Communists are in no way based on ideas or principles that have been invented or discovered by this or that would-be universal reformer. They merely express, in general terms, actual relations springing from an existing class struggle, from a historical movement going on under our very eyes.

The abolition of existing property relations is not at all a distinctive feature of communism. All property relations in the past have continually been subject to historical change consequent upon the change in historical conditions. The French Revolution, for example, abolished feudal property in favor of bourgeois property. The distinguishing feature of communism is not the abolition of property generally, but the abolition of bourgeois property. But modern bourgeois private property is the final and most complete expression of the system of producing and appropriating products that is based on class antagonisms, on the exploitation of the many by the few. In this sense, the theory of the Communists may be summed up in the single thought: abolition of private property.

We Communists have been reproached with the desire of abolishing the right of personally acquiring property as the fruit of a man's own labor, which property is alleged to be the groundwork of all personal freedom, activity, and independence. Hard-won, self-acquired, self-earned property! Do you mean the property of petty artisan and of the small peasant, a form of property that preceded the bourgeois form? There is no need to abolish that; the development of industry has to a great extent already destroyed it and is still destroying it daily. Or do you mean the modern bourgeois private property?

But does wage labor create any property for the laborer? Not a bit. It creates capital—that kind of property which exploits wage labor and which cannot increase except upon conditions of begetting a new supply of wage labor for fresh exploitation. Property, in its present form, is based on the antagonism of capital and wage labor. Let us examine both sides of this antagonism.

To be a capitalist is to have not only a purely personal, but also a social status in production. Capital is a collective product, and only by the united action of many members, nay, in the last resort, only by the united action of all members of society, can it be set in motion. Capital is therefore not only personal; it is a social power. When, therefore, capital is converted into common property, into the property of all members of society, personal property is not thereby transformed into social property. It is only the social character of the property that is changed. It loses its class character.

Let us now take wage labor. The average price of wage labor is the minimum wage, i.e., that quantum of the means of subsistence, which is absolutely requisite to keep the laborer in bare existence as a laborer. What, therefore, the wage laborer appropriates by means of his labor merely suffices to prolong and reproduce a bare existence. We by no means intend to abolish this personal appropriation of the products of labor, an appropriation that is made for the maintenance and reproduction of human life, and that leaves no surplus wherewith to command the labor of others. All that we want to do away with is the miserable character of this appropriation, under which the laborer lives merely to increase capital, and is allowed to live only in so far as the interest of the ruling class requires it...

You are horrified at our intending to do away with private property. But in your existing society, private property is already done away with for nine-tenths of the population; its existence for the few is solely due to its non-existence in the hands of those nine-tenths. You reproach us, therefore, with intending to do away with a form of property, the necessary condition for whose existence is the non-existence of any property for the immense majority of society. In one word, you reproach us with intending to do away with your property. Precisely so, that is just what we intend...

It has been objected that upon the abolition of private property, all work will cease, and universal laziness will overtake us. According to this, bourgeois society ought long ago to have gone to the dogs through sheer idleness, for those who acquire anything, do not work. The whole of this objection is but another expression of the tautology: There can no longer be any wage labor when there is no longer any capital.

All objections urged against the communistic mode of producing and appropriating material products, have, in the same way, been urged against the communistic mode of producing and appropriating intellectual products. Just as to the bourgeois, the disappearance of class property is the disappearance of production itself, so the disappearance of class culture is to him identical with the disappearance of all culture.

That culture, the loss of which he laments, is, for the enormous majority, a mere training to act as a machine. But don't wrangle with us so long as you apply, to our intended abolition of bourgeois property, the standard of your bourgeois notions of freedom, culture, law, etc. Your very ideas are but the outgrowth of the conditions of your bourgeois production and bourgeois property, just as your jurisprudence is but the will of your class made into a law for all, a will whose essential character and direction are determined by the economical conditions of existence of your class. The selfish misconception that induces you to transform into eternal laws of nature and of reason the social forms stringing from your present mode of production and form of property—historical relations that rise and disappear in the progress of production—this misconception you share with every ruling class that has preceded you. What you see clearly in the case of ancient property, what you admit in the case of feudal property, you are of course forbidden to admit in the case of your own bourgeois form of property.

Abolition of the family! Even the most radical flare up at this infamous proposal of the Communists. On what foundation is the present family, the bourgeois family, based? On capital, on private gain. In its completely developed form, this family exists only among the bourgeoisie. But this state of things finds its complement in the practical absence of the family among proletarians, and in public prostitution. The bourgeois family will vanish as a matter of course when its complement vanishes, and both will vanish with the vanishing of capital.

Do you charge us with wanting to stop the exploitation of children by their parents? To this crime we plead guilty. But, you say, we destroy the most hallowed of relations, when we replace home education by social education. And your education! Is not that also social, and determined by the social conditions under which you educate, by the intervention direct or indirect, of society, by means of schools, etc.? The Communists have not intended the intervention of society in education; they do but seek to alter the character of that intervention, and to rescue education from the influence of the ruling class.

The bourgeois claptrap about the family and education, about the hallowed correlation of parents and child, becomes all the more disgusting the more...all the family ties among the proletarians are torn asunder, and their children transformed into simple articles of commerce and instruments of labor...

The Communists are further reproached with desiring to abolish countries and nationality. The workingmen have no country. We cannot take from them what they have not got. ...National differences and antagonism between peoples are daily more and more vanishing, owing to the development of the bourgeoisie, to freedom of commerce, to the world market, to uniformity in the mode of production and in the conditions of life corresponding thereto. The supremacy of the proletariat will cause them to vanish still faster. United action of the leading civilized countries at least is one of the first conditions for the emancipation of the proletariat. In proportion as the exploitation of one individual by another will also be put to an end, the exploitation of one nation by another will also be put to an end. In proportion as the antagonism between classes within the nation vanishes, the hostility of one nation to another will come to an end.

The charges against communism made from a religious, a philosophical and, generally, from an ideological standpoint, are not deserving of serious examination. Does it require deep intuition to comprehend that man's ideas, views, and conception, in one word, man's consciousness, changes with every change in the conditions of his material existence, in his social relations and in his social life? What else does the history of ideas prove, than that intellectual production changes its character in proportion as material production is changed?

The ruling ideas of each age have ever been the ideas of its ruling class. When people speak of the ideas that revolutionize society, they do but express that fact that within the old society the elements of a new one have been created, and that the dissolution of the old ideas keeps even pace with the dissolution of the old conditions of existence.

When the ancient world was in its last throes, the ancient religions were overcome by Christianity. When Christian ideas succumbed in the eighteenth century to rationalist ideas, feudal society fought its death battle with the then revolutionary bourgeoisie. The ideas of religious liberty and freedom of conscience merely gave expression to the sway of free competition within the domain of knowledge.

"Undoubtedly," it will be said, "religious, moral, philosophical, and juridical ideas have been modified in the course of historical development. But religion, morality, philosophy, political science, and law, constantly survived this change. There are, besides, eternal truths, such as freedom, justice, etc., that are common to all states of society. But communism abolishes eternal truths, it abolishes all religion, and all morality, instead of constituting them on a new basis; it therefore acts in contradiction to all past historical experience."

What does this accusation reduce itself to? The history of all past society has consisted in the development of class antagonisms, antagonisms that assumed different forms at different epochs. But whatever form they may have taken, one fact is common to all past ages: the exploitation of one part of society by the other. No wonder, then, that the social consciousness of past ages, despite all the multiplicity and variety it displays, moves within certain common forms, or general ideas, which cannot completely vanish except with the total disappearance of class antagonisms. The communist revolution is the most radical rupture with traditional relations; no wonder that its development involved the most radical rupture with traditional ideas.

But let us be done with the bourgeois objections to communism. We have seen above that the first step in the revolution by the working class is to raise the proletariat to the position of ruling class to win the battle of democracy. The proletariat will use its political supremacy to wrest, by degree, all capital from the bourgeoisie, to centralize all instruments of production in the hands of the state, i.e., of the proletariat organized as the ruling class; and to increase the total productive forces as rapidly as possible.

Of course, in the beginning, this cannot be effected except by means of despotic inroads on the rights of property, and on the conditions of bourgeois production; by means of measures, therefore, which appear economically insufficient and untenable, but which, in the course of the movement, outstrip themselves, necessitate further inroads upon the old social order, and are unavoidable as a means of entirely revolutionizing the mode of production.

These measures will, of course, be different in different countries. Nevertheless, in most advanced countries, the following will be pretty generally applicable.

1. Abolition of property in land; application of all rents of land to public purposes.
2. A heavy progressive or graduated income tax.
3. Abolition of all rights of inheritance.
4. Confiscation of the property of all emigrants and rebels.
5. Centralization of credit in the banks of the state, by means of a national bank; an exclusive monopoly on setting interest rates.
6. Centralization of the means of communication and transportation in the hands of the state.
7. Extension of factories and means of production owned by the state; the bringing into cultivation of wastelands; the improvement of the soil generally in accordance with a common plan.
8. Equal obligation of all to work; establishment of industrial armies, especially for agriculture.
9. Combination of agriculture with manufacturing industries; gradual abolition of all the distinction between town and country by a more equable distribution of the populace over the country.
10. Free education for all children in public schools; abolition of children's factory labor in its present form; combination of education with industrial production, etc.

When, in the course of development, class distinctions have disappeared, and all production has been concentrated in the hands of a vast association of the whole nation, the public power will lose its political character. Political power, properly so called, is merely the organized power of one class for oppressing another.

If the proletariat during its contest with the bourgeoisie is compelled, by the force of circumstances, to organize itself as a class; if, by means of a revolution, it makes itself the ruling class, and, as such, sweeps away by force the old conditions of production, then it will, along with these conditions, have swept away the conditions for the existence of class antagonisms and of classes generally, and will thereby have abolished its own supremacy as a class.

In place of the old bourgeois society, with its classes and class antagonisms, we shall have an association in which the free development of each is the condition for the free development of all...

The Communists everywhere support every revolutionary movement against the existing social and political order of things. In all these movements, they bring to the front, as the leading question in each, the property question, no matter what its degree of development at the time.

Finally, they labor everywhere for the union and agreement of the democratic parties of all countries. The Communists disdain to conceal their views and aims. They openly declare that their ends can be attained only by the forcible overthrow of all existing social conditions. Let the ruling classes tremble at a communist revolution. The proletarians have nothing to lose but their chains. They have a world to win.

Working men of all countries, unite!

QUESTIONS FOR REVIEW/DISCUSSION:

➢ Early in this essay Marx talks about the economic and intellectual interdependence of nations as though it is a bad thing when it happens. What is economic and intellectual interdependence and is it bad?

➢ Marx refers to wage labor as though it is a most distasteful way to make a living; he even says that when capitalism is destroyed wage labor will be destroyed. How will people earn a living? How will they be paid in the communist society? Does he address these questions?

➤ Go back and read again the ten points Marx makes about what will have to be done when the proletariat takes control. What do you think about the items on this list?

XII. Andrew Carnegie:
The Gospel of Wealth

Andrew Carnegie (1835-1919) was one of those men from the late 1800s and early 1900s known collectively as 'Robber Barons' or 'Captains of Industry'—depending on your perspective. No matter which name you choose, they all left a lasting imprint on American capitalism—and in the process became filthy rich. But they did something else in the process of acquiring wealth; they increased the standard of living of all Americans by providing services and products that ultimately made everyone's life easier and businesses more productive and efficient. They were all believers in Adam Smith's philosophy of enlightened self-interest.

Carnegie originally emigrated from Scotland as a young boy. He made his money from railroads, oil, and eventually iron and steel production. In 1901 he sold the Carnegie Steel Company, which controlled about 25 percent of the total U.S. steel production, to the U.S. Steel Corporation and retired. He spent the rest of his life giving away his millions.

Carnegie was one of the greatest philanthropists this world has ever seen. He felt that one was obligated, indeed required, to give back to that society which had given him so much. This is what came to be known as the Gospel of Wealth. During his lifetime Carnegie gave away $350 million to various cultural and educational organizations and ventures. Many of his contemporaries—his fellow Robber Barons—also gave away large amounts of money in other various philanthropic ventures. In that way, not only did they raise the living standard of society in general but they also used their own money made from their business ventures to "spread the wealth around" a little bit.

Andrew Carnegie: The Gospel Of Wealth

The Socialist or Anarchist who seeks to overturn present conditions is to be regarded as attacking the foundation upon which civilization itself rests, for civilization took its start from the day that the capable, industrious workman said to his incompetent and lazy fellow, "If thou dost not sow, thou shalt not reap," and thus ended primitive communism by separating the drones from the bees. One who studies this subject will soon be brought face to face with the conclusion that upon the sacredness of property civilization itself depends—the right of the laborer to his hundred dollars in the savings bank, and equally the legal right of the millionaire to his millions. To those who propose to substitute communism for this intense individualism the answer, therefore, is: the race has tried that. All progress from that barbarous day to the present time has resulted from its displacement. Not evil, but good, has come to the race from the accumulation of wealth by those who have the ability and energy that produce it.

We might as well urge the destruction of the highest existing type of man because he failed to reach our ideal as to favor the destruction of Individualism, Private Property, the Law of Accumulation of Wealth, and the Law of Competition; for these are the highest results of human experience, the soil in which society so far has produced the best fruit. Unequally or unjustly, perhaps, as these laws sometimes operate, and imperfect as they appear to the idealist, they are, nevertheless, like the highest type of man, the best and most valuable of all that humanity has yet accomplished.

We start, then, with a condition of affairs under which the best interests of the race are promoted, but which inevitably gives wealth to the few. Thus far, accepting conditions as they exist, the situation can be surveyed and pronounced good. The question then arises, and, if the foregoing be correct, it is the only question with which we have to deal: What is the proper mode of administering wealth after the laws upon which civilization is founded have thrown it into the hands of the few? And it is of this great question that I believe I offer the true solution. It will be understood that fortunes are here spoken of, not moderate sums saved by many years of effort, the returns from which are required for the comfortable maintenance and education of families. This is not wealth, but only competence, which it should be the aim of all to acquire.

There are but three modes in which surplus wealth can be disposed of. It can be left to the families of the decedents; or it can be bequeathed for public purposes; or, finally, it can be administered during their lives by its possessors. Under the first and second modes most of the wealth of the world that has reached the few has hitherto been applied. Let us in turn consider each of these modes. The first is the most injudicious. In monarchical countries, the estates and the greatest portion of the wealth are left to the first son, that the vanity of the parent may be gratified by the thought that his name and title are to descend to succeeding generations unimpaired. The condition of this class in Europe today teaches the futility of such hopes or ambitions. The successors have become impoverished through their follies or from the fall in the value of land. Even in Great Britain the strict law of entail has been found inadequate to maintain the status of an hereditary class. Its soil is rapidly passing into the hands of the stranger. Under republican institutions the division of property among the children is much fairer, but the question, which forces itself upon thoughtful men in all lands, is: Why should men leave great fortunes to their children? If this is done from affection, is it not misguided affection?

Observation teaches that, generally speaking, it is not well for the children to be so burdened. It is not suggested that men who have failed to educate their sons to earn a livelihood shall cast them adrift in poverty. If any man has seen fit to rear his sons with a view to their living idle lives, or, what is highly commendable, has instilled in them the sentiment that they are in a position to labor for public ends without reference to pecuniary considerations, then, of course, the duty of the parent is to see that such are provided for in moderation. There are instances of millionaires' sons unspoiled by wealth, who, being rich, still perform great services in the community. Such are the very salt of the earth, as valuable as, unfortunately, they are rare; still it is not the exception but the rule that men must regard, and, looking at the usual result of enormous sums conferred upon legatees, the thoughtful man must shortly say, "I would as soon leave to my son a curse as the almighty dollar," and admit to himself that it is not the welfare of the children but family pride which inspires these enormous legacies.

As to the second mode, that of leaving wealth at death for public uses, it may be said that this is only a means for the disposal of wealth, provided a man is content to wait until he is dead before it becomes of much good in the world. Knowledge of the results of legacies bequeathed is not calculated to inspire the brightest hopes of much posthumous good being accomplished. The cases are not few in which the real object sought by the testator is not attained, nor are they few in which his real wishes are thwarted. In many cases the bequests are so used as to become only monuments of his folly. It is well to remember that it requires the exercise of not less ability than that which acquired the wealth to use it so as to be really beneficial to the community. Besides this, it may fairly be said that no man is to be extolled for doing what he cannot help doing, nor is he to be thanked by the community to which he only leaves wealth at death. Men who leave vast sums in this way may fairly be thought men who would not have left it at all, had they been able to take it with them. The memories of such cannot be held in grateful remembrance, for there is no grace in their gifts. It is not to be wondered at that such bequests seem so generally to lack the blessing.

The growing disposition to tax more and more heavily large estates left at death is a cheering indication of the growth of a salutary change in public opinion. The State of Pennsylvania now takes—subject to some exceptions—one-tenth of the property left by its citizens. The budget presented in the British Parliament the other day proposes to increase the death duties; and, most significant of all, the new tax is to be a graduated one. Of all forms of taxation, this seems the wisest. Men who continue hoarding great sums all their lives, the proper use of which for public ends would work good to the community, should be made to feel that the community, in the form of the state, cannot thus be deprived of its proper share. By taxing estates heavily at death the state marks its condemnation of the selfish millionaire's unworthy life.

There remains, then, only one mode of using great fortunes; but in this we have the true antidote for the temporary unequal distribution of wealth, the reconciliation of the rich and the poor—a reign of harmony—another ideal, differing indeed from that of the communist in requiring only the further evolution of existing conditions, not the total overthrow of our civilization. It is founded upon the present most intense individualism, and the race is prepared to put it in practice by degrees whenever it pleases. Under its sway we shall have an ideal state in which the surplus wealth of the few will become, in the best sense, the property of the many because it is administered for the common good, and this wealth passing through the hands of the few can be made a much more potent force for the elevation of our race than if it had been distributed in small sums to the people themselves. Even the poorest can be made to see this and to agree that great sums gathered by some of their fellow-citizens and spent for public purposes, from which the masses reap the principal benefit, are more valuable to them than if scattered among them through the course of many years in trifling amounts.

Poor and restricted are our opportunities in this life, narrow our horizon, our best work most imperfect, but rich men should be thankful for one inestimable boon. They have it in their power during their lives to busy themselves in organizing benefactions from which the masses of their fellows will derive lasting advantage, and thus dignify their own lives.

QUESTIONS FOR THOUGHT/DISCUSSION:

> Look up the definitions of the words primogenitor and entail. Carnegie would not agree that these are good things. Why not?

> Carnegie opines that there are three things a millionaire can do with his money. Which does he believe is the best choice and why?

> Carnegie makes several comparisons between communism and capitalism. Why does he believe communism would be a failure?

Index

America, 3, 5, 6, 17, 44, 45, 52-54, 56, 58, 61, 101, 139, 143, 144

anarchy, 7, 52

Aquinas, Thomas 7, 85, 86, 93

aristocracy, 4, 44, 45, 47, 48, 61, 65-67, 71-73, 82, 88, 90, 91

Aristotle, 4, 6, 62, 63, 84, 85, 92

army, 97, 98, 147

assembly, 9, 11, 14, 29, 70, 74, 78, 82, 116

Bentham, Jeremy 101, 142

Bill of Rights, 34

bourgeoisie, 143-150, 153, 155, 157

capital, 98, 100, 121, 131-133, 137, 138, 144, 147, 148, 150-153, 155, 156

capitalism, 2, 4, 7, 8, 61, 126, 127, 142, 157, 159, 163

capitalist, 2, 7, 8, 63, 142, 147, 151

capitalists, 8, 143, 148

Carnegie, Andres 8, 159, 163

children, 20, 21, 25, 52, 89, 119-125, 153, 154, 156, 161

Churchill, Winston 5

Cicero, Marcus 7, 92, 94, 100

civilization, 9, 114, 123, 146, 160, 163

commerce, 68, 131, 137-139, 144, 147, 154

commonwealth, 19, 23, 28-32, 72, 96, 97

communism, 2, 4, 7, 8, 142, 151, 154, 155, 160, 163

Communists, 142, 150, 151, 153, 154, 157

consent of the governed, 2, 4, 17

constitution, 3, 9, 13, 43, 46, 59, 64-66, 70-78, 83, 102, 104, 108, 109, 124

constitutional government, 65, 72-75, 79

courts, 80, 82, 83, 100

Democracy in America, 44

divine right of kings, 4, 17

economic, 2, 6, 7, 63, 126, 141, 157

economic policy, 2

economy, 1, 2, 126, 127

education, 4, 6, 71-75, 119, 120, 125, 129, 130, 153, 156, 160

egalitarian, 6

elect, 74, 78, 99

Engels, Frederick, 141

England, 17, 25, 48, 53, 121, 132, 133, 138

enlightened, 4, 6, 8, 11, 17, 38, 42, 46, 48, 109, 124, 126, 142, 159

Enlightened Era, 17, 126

equality, 11, 23, 27, 40, 57, 59, 63, 66, 69, 74, 77, 78, 94, 110, 111

Europe, 51, 53, 85, 135, 136, 140, 142, 161

evil, 35, 45, 48, 56, 61, 75, 90, 91, 92, 102, 104, 117, 123, 136, 160

faction, 35-42, 76

factions, 10, 11, 35, 37, 43, 76, 84

France, 17, 25, 44, 53, 132-139

freedom, 2, 5, 9, 18, 21, 25, 30, 58, 68, 73, 105, 114, 122, 135, 151, 153-155

Fukuyama, Francis 2, 6

Great Britain, 135, 137-139, 161

Greece, 5, 62
Hegel, 2, 141
individualism, 160, 163
industry, 133, 137, 138, 144, 145-151
injustice, 26, 35, 36, 39, 42, 111, 121, 136
Jefferson, Thomas 6, 7, 18, 34
judges, 28, 30, 38, 70, 73, 80, 83, 96, 98, 100
judgment, 38, 103, 115, 138
judicial, 38, 78, 82
justice, 4, 7, 26, 30, 36-40, 62, 69, 73, 83, 88, 92, 95-100, 117, 155
king, 7, 49, 65, 86, 89, 90, 93, 117
labor, 27, 36, 48, 126, 127, 129, 131, 134, 140, 141, 144, 147, 148, 150-152, 154, 156, 157, 161
law, 2, 4, 7, 11, 12, 14, 17, 18, 21, 25-33, 38, 44, 45, 55, 56, 58, 63, 69-71, 79-83, 92, 94-101, 105, 120, 126, 141, 149, 153, 155, 161
legislation, 38, 45, 48, 55, 56, 59, 78, 110
legislative, 27-32, 38, 56, 57
legislators, 29, 38, 77
liberal, 2, 3, 48
liberalism, 2, 126
liberty, 3, 5, 7, 13, 15-19, 24, 25-29, 30, 35-37, 54, 57, 59, 69, 99, 105, 114, 155
literacy, 6
Locke, John 4, 7, 10, 17, 18, 33
Madison, James 4, 34, 35, 43, 84, 93
magistrate, 23, 30, 46-48, 53, 81, 96-99
magistrates, 48, 64, 69-71, 78-80, 82, 83, 96-100
majoritarian, 3, 7, 61, 94

majority, 3-6, 13-15, 17-19, 32, 36, 39-42, 45-48, 55, 56, 61, 63, 67, 70-75, 80, 93, 95, 102, 110-115, 117, 120, 152, 153
Mann, Horace 6, 119, 124, 125
market, 82, 126, 131, 137, 139, 144-147, 154
Marx, Karl 6, 7, 8, 141, 142, 157, 158
Marxism, 8, 141, 142
Middle Ages, 85, 143-145
middle class, 63, 75-77, 84, 144, 148
Mill, John Stuart 4, 6, 7, 101, 102, 117, 118, 142
minority, 3, 5, 6, 35, 36, 44, 45, 55, 61, 93, 102, 108, 111-115, 117, 122
monarchy, 4, 17, 22, 24, 49, 50, 65, 70-73, 82, 91, 104
money, 12, 42, 106, 128, 145, 159, 163
morality, 9, 47, 50, 53, 95, 155
natural rights, 4, 17, 18, 94
Newton, Isaac 4
oligarchy, 64-69, 71-79, 82, 88, 91
On The Laws, 94
Parliament, 101, 112, 113, 162
party, 12, 36-42, 55, 71, 77, 99, 108, 113, 142, 150
pleasure, 1, 31, 42, 58, 101
politicians, 40
politics, 1, 3, 57, 62, 80, 101, 107, 113, 137
poor, 6, 32, 47, 48, 53, 56, 66-71, 73-77, 80, 120, 134, 137, 138, 162
popular government, 5, 106
popular opinion, 3, 110, 116, 117
proletariat, 143, 147-150, 154-158

property, 5, 6, 21, 22, 26-32,
    37-42, 53, 54, 59, 63, 66,
    69-71, 74, 76, 92, 98, 108,
    145, 146, 151-157, 160-163
public good, 12, 23, 28-29, 36-
    40
public opinion, 3, 106, 162
religion, 4, 37, 49, 50, 155
Report On The Public
    Schools, 119
representative government,
    17, 35
republic, 5, 9, 13, 40-44, 50,
    94, 104
republicanism, 5
rich, 6, 32, 47, 48, 53, 56, 66,
    67, 69, 72-77, 80, 81, 88,
    92, 137-140, 159-163
Roman Empire, 94
Rousseau, Jean Jacques 4, 9,
    10, 15, 16
royalty, 4
rule of law, 7, 44
ruler, 22, 23, 31, 67, 88, 92,
    136
Russia, 109
Ryn, Claus 3
schools, 119, 123
science, 45, 63, 103, 144, 155
self-interest, 1, 4, 8, 126, 142,
    159
Smith, Adam 7, 8, 126, 127,
    140, 159
social compact, 14
state of nature, 9, 18-20, 25-
    30

Stoicism, 94
taxation, 146, 162
taxes, 32, 38
The Communist Manifesto,
    141
The Gospel Of Wealth, 8, 159
The Governance Of Rulers, 86
The Politics, 62
The Social Contract, 9
The Wealth of Nations, 8, 126
theology, 85
Toqueville, Alexis de 1, 5, 6,
    44, 45, 61, 101
trade, 68, 127, 131, 132, 133,
    134, 135, 137, 138, 139,
    140, 143, 148
tyranny, 3-5, 35, 44, 52, 61,
    65, 70, 72, 76, 79, 88, 90,
    91, 93, 106
U.S. House of
    Representatives, 119
United States, 6, 7, 34, 46, 47,
    49, 51, 52, 55-59, 113
Utilitarianism, 101
virtue, 23, 46, 52, 54, 62, 65,
    73, 75, 92, 94, 99, 117, 122
vote, 6, 10, 12, 14, 15, 16, 39,
    43, 55, 78-83, 106, 113, 115
voting, 5, 6, 13, 15, 55, 117
wealth, 5, 20, 27, 30, 32, 45,
    53, 56, 66, 68, 72, 73, 75,
    92, 126, 137-142, 149, 159-
    162

ABOUT THE AUTHOR

Maryann Zihala is a political scientist, U.S. Air Force veteran, and the author of Edith Wharton's Old New York Society (2002). She holds a B.A. in political science from the University of Maryland, a M.A. in international relations from the Catholic University of America, and a J.D. from Southern California University. She teaches political science, history, and criminal justice.